ST. JOHN

TRAVEL GUIDE 2025:

Explore the Island's Best Beaches, Hiking Trails, and Hidden Gems in the Virgin Islands.

BY

Martin C. Scott

CONTENT

MAP OF ST. JOHN

St. John

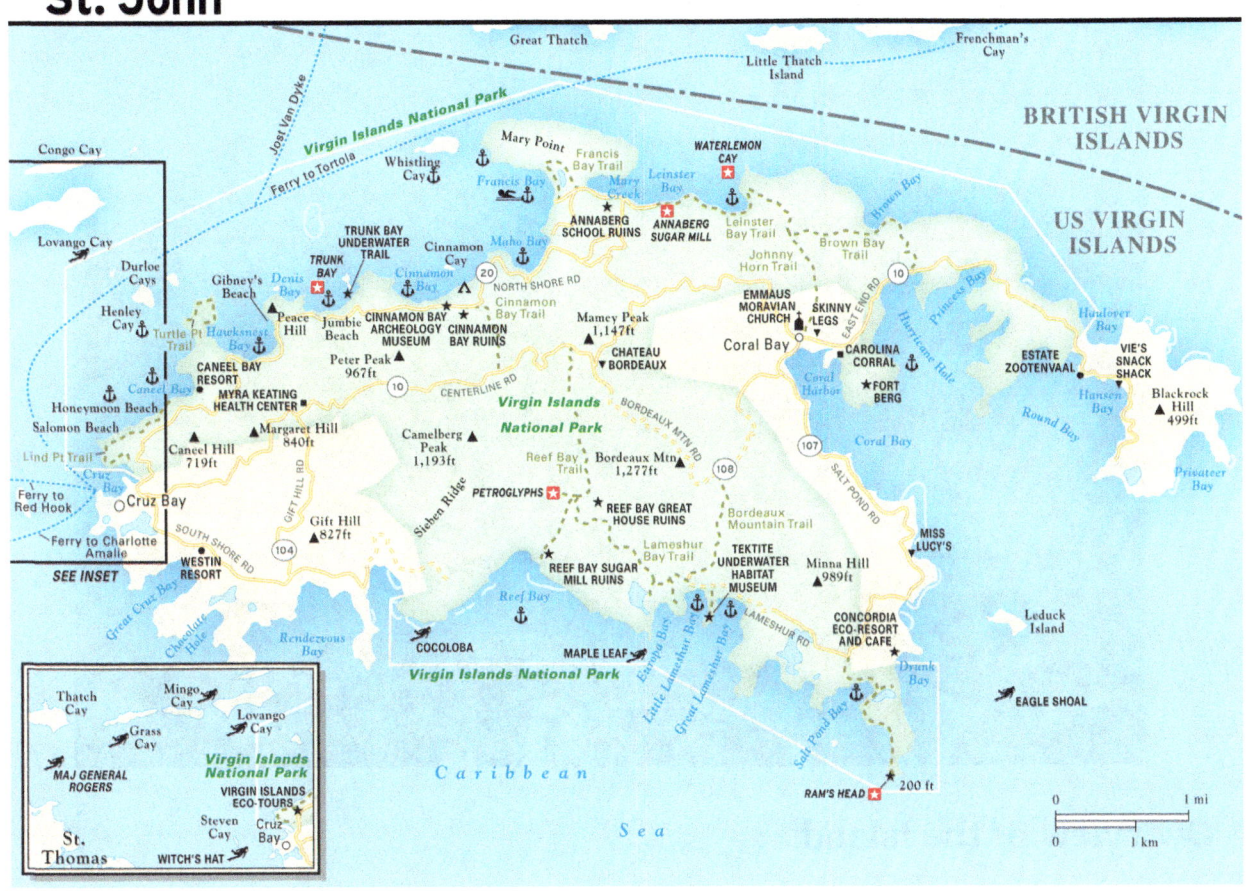

Introduction

Overview of the Island

St. John, the smallest of the three main U.S. Virgin Islands, is a Caribbean paradise known for its pristine beaches, lush tropical landscapes, and rich cultural heritage. Covering an area of just 20 square miles, it offers an intimate escape that combines natural beauty with vibrant island culture. Unlike its bustling neighbors, St. Thomas and St. Croix, St. John remains largely undeveloped, thanks to the Virgin Islands National Park, which protects nearly two-thirds of the island.

St. John's history is steeped in a blend of African, European, and Indigenous influences, reflected in its architecture, traditions, and cuisine. Once a Danish colony, the island's sugar plantations now serve as historical landmarks, telling the story of its complex past. Today, St. John is celebrated as a haven for eco-tourists, nature enthusiasts, and those seeking tranquility amidst unspoiled surroundings.

The island's main settlements, Cruz Bay and Coral Bay, offer distinct vibes. Cruz Bay, often referred to as the "gateway to St. John," is a lively hub filled with boutique shops, waterfront restaurants, and cultural sites. Coral Bay, on the other hand, provides a quieter, more rustic experience, appealing to visitors seeking solitude and connection with nature.

Why Visit St. John in 2025?

As the world embraces travel again, St. John is emerging as a top destination for 2025, offering unparalleled experiences that blend relaxation, adventure, and sustainability. Here's why St. John should be at the top of your travel list this year:

1. **Renewed Focus on Sustainable Tourism**
   - St. John is committed to preserving its natural beauty, with initiatives aimed at protecting coral reefs, reducing plastic waste, and promoting eco-friendly tourism. Visitors in 2025 can enjoy the island while knowing their trip contributes to conservation efforts.
2. **Exciting Events and Celebrations**
   - In 2025, the island will host a series of cultural festivals, including the St. John Carnival, a vibrant display of music, dance, and local traditions. These events offer a unique opportunity to immerse yourself in the island's rich heritage.
3. **Reinvigorated Hospitality Sector**
   - The post-pandemic revival has seen the reopening of luxury resorts, boutique hotels, and local businesses, many of which have undergone upgrades to enhance visitor experiences.
4. **Virgin Islands National Park's 70th Anniversary**
   - Celebrating seven decades of conservation, the park will host special guided tours, educational programs, and community events, making 2025 a perfect year to explore its wonders.
5. **Accessibility and Convenience**
   - With improved ferry schedules and direct flights to nearby St. Thomas, reaching St. John has never been easier. Travelers can enjoy seamless connections from major U.S. cities.

Quick Facts and Highlights

Here's a snapshot of what makes St. John a must-visit destination:

- **Location**: Part of the U.S. Virgin Islands in the Caribbean, east of St. Thomas.
- **Size**: Approximately 20 square miles.
- **Population**: Around 4,000 residents.
- **Currency**: U.S. Dollar (USD).
- **Language**: English, with some residents speaking Creole or Spanish.

- **Entry Requirements**: As a U.S. territory, no passport is required for U.S. citizens, but valid ID is needed.
- **Climate**: Tropical, with temperatures averaging 77°F to 84°F year-round.
- **National Park Coverage**: 60% of the island, including beaches, trails, and historical sites.
- **Famous Beaches**: Trunk Bay, Cinnamon Bay, Honeymoon Beach.
- **Signature Activities**: Snorkeling, hiking, sailing, and exploring historical ruins.
- **Wildlife**: Home to endangered species like sea turtles, brown pelicans, and coral reefs teeming with marine life.
- **Unique Features**:
    - The Annaberg Plantation ruins, a window into the island's colonial history.
    - Reef Bay Trail, where you can discover petroglyphs carved by the Taino people.
    - Coral Bay, known for its bohemian charm and laid-back ambiance.

St. John's unspoiled beauty and dedication to sustainability make it an unmatched destination for 2025. Whether you're looking to bask in the sun on world-renowned beaches, explore vibrant marine ecosystems, or delve into the island's storied past, St. John promises an unforgettable escape.

Getting to St. John

St. John, with its serene beaches and lush landscapes, is a sought-after destination in the U.S. Virgin Islands. While its remote nature adds to its charm, it also requires careful planning to reach. This chapter provides comprehensive details about transportation options, the best times to travel, entry requirements, and essential travel tips, ensuring a seamless journey to this Caribbean paradise.

Transportation Options

Traveling to St. John involves a combination of air and sea transportation. As the island lacks its own airport, visitors must first arrive in nearby St. Thomas and then take a ferry or private charter to St. John. Here are the key transportation options:

Flights to St. Thomas

The closest airport to St. John is the Cyril E. King Airport (STT) on St. Thomas, located approximately 13 miles away from St. John.

- **Airlines**: Major airlines such as American Airlines, Delta, United, JetBlue, and Spirit offer flights to St. Thomas from major U.S. cities, including Miami, Atlanta, Charlotte, New York, and Dallas.

- **Pricing**: Round-trip fares typically range from $300 to $800, depending on the season and departure city. Booking in advance often results in better rates.
- **Arrival Tips**: Once you land in St. Thomas, you can take a taxi to one of the ferry terminals: either Red Hook or Charlotte Amalie. Taxi rides from Cyril E. King Airport to Red Hook cost approximately $15-$20 per person, while the ride to Charlotte Amalie is about $10-$15 per person.

Ferries to St. John

The ferry is the most popular and cost-effective way to travel from St. Thomas to St. John. Two main ferry routes connect the islands:

1. **Red Hook to Cruz Bay**
   - **Duration**: 20 minutes.
   - **Frequency**: Ferries operate every hour from early morning to late evening.
   - **Pricing**: Adults: $8 one-way; Children: $1. Baggage fees are $4 per bag.
   - **Convenience**: Red Hook is a 30-minute taxi ride from Cyril E. King Airport and is the most frequently used terminal for St. John ferries.
2. **Charlotte Amalie to Cruz Bay**
   - **Duration**: 40 minutes.
   - **Frequency**: Fewer departures compared to Red Hook. Ideal for travelers staying near the airport or downtown Charlotte Amalie.
   - **Pricing**: Adults: $12 one-way; Children: $6.

Private Charters

For those seeking a more exclusive and direct journey, private boat charters are an excellent option.

- **Operators**: Popular charter companies include Dolphin Water Taxi and Island Time Charters.
- **Pricing**: Private charters start at around $250 for a group of four, with additional costs for extra passengers.
- **Advantages**: Flexible schedules, personalized service, and the ability to enjoy a scenic ride through the Caribbean waters.

Car Rentals and Water Taxis

While St. John is accessible by ferry, travelers renting vehicles on St. Thomas may need a car barge.

- **Car Barge Services**: Operates between Red Hook and St. John. Round-trip costs approximately $50–$75.
- **Water Taxis**: For late-night arrivals, water taxis are available. Pricing starts at $150 per trip.

Best Times to Travel

Choosing the right time to visit St. John can greatly enhance your experience. The island's tropical climate ensures warm weather year-round, but seasonal variations affect crowd levels, costs, and activities.

Peak Season (December to April)

- **Weather**: Sunny and dry, with average temperatures between 77°F and 84°F.
- **Crowds**: High; popular beaches and accommodations may be busier.
- **Advantages**: Ideal for escaping cold winters and enjoying events like the St. John Carnival.
- **Pricing**: Accommodation rates are at their highest, with luxury resorts charging $500–$1,000 per night. Booking several months in advance is recommended.

Shoulder Season (May to June)

- **Weather**: Warm and slightly humid.
- **Crowds**: Moderate; fewer tourists than peak season.
- **Advantages**: Lower hotel rates (starting at $200 per night), making it a budget-friendly time to visit. Excellent conditions for snorkeling and hiking.
- **Events**: St. John Festival, celebrated in late June, is a major highlight.

Off-Season (July to November)

- **Weather**: Hot and humid, with an increased risk of hurricanes from August to October.
- **Crowds**: Low; the island is quieter, and some businesses may close temporarily.
- **Advantages**: Significantly lower travel costs, with accommodations starting at $150 per night. Perfect for travelers seeking solitude and tranquility.
- **Cautions**: Monitor weather updates and purchase travel insurance during this period.

Entry Requirements and Travel Tips

Getting to St. John involves navigating specific entry requirements and understanding local travel norms. These guidelines will help ensure a smooth journey:

Entry Requirements

As a U.S. territory, entry procedures for St. John are straightforward for U.S. citizens and international visitors.

- **U.S. Citizens**:
  - No passport is required.
  - A government-issued photo ID (e.g., driver's license) is sufficient.
- **International Travelers**:
  - Must have a valid passport and, depending on nationality, a U.S. visa or ESTA (Electronic System for Travel Authorization) for eligible countries.
- **COVID-19 Guidelines**:
  - As of 2025, no specific COVID-19 restrictions are in place, but it's advisable to check for updates before travel.

Travel Tips for a Smooth Journey

1. **Pack Light**
   - Many ferries and private charters charge extra for large luggage. Opt for carry-ons when possible.
2. **Stay Informed About Ferry Schedules**
   - Ferry times may change due to weather conditions. Confirm schedules with operators before your trip.
3. **Cash is King**
   - While credit cards are accepted in most places, taxis, ferries, and small shops often prefer cash. Bring small bills for tips and payments.
4. **Use Sunscreen and Bug Repellent**
   - The tropical climate necessitates protection against the sun and mosquitoes. Reef-safe sunscreen is encouraged to protect marine life.
5. **Pre-Book Rentals and Excursions**
   - Whether renting a car or booking a snorkeling tour, securing reservations in advance ensures availability during busy periods.
6. **Stay Connected**
   - While Wi-Fi is available in most accommodations, consider a local SIM card or an international roaming plan for seamless communication.

Where to Stay in St. John

St. John is a haven for travelers seeking diverse accommodation options that cater to all preferences and budgets. From luxurious resorts perched on cliffside vistas to cozy family-friendly villas and budget-conscious rentals, the island provides a perfect setting for every type of traveler. Understanding the island's layout, key regions, and unique charm of each area will help you find your ideal base for an unforgettable stay.

Top Luxury Resorts

For those who desire a stay that exudes opulence, St. John's luxury resorts offer unparalleled comfort, exceptional amenities, and breathtaking views. These high-end properties are primarily located near Cruz Bay, the island's bustling town center, providing easy access to upscale dining, shopping, and transportation hubs.

Caneel Bay Resort

- **Location**: Nestled within the Virgin Islands National Park, just a short drive from Cruz Bay.

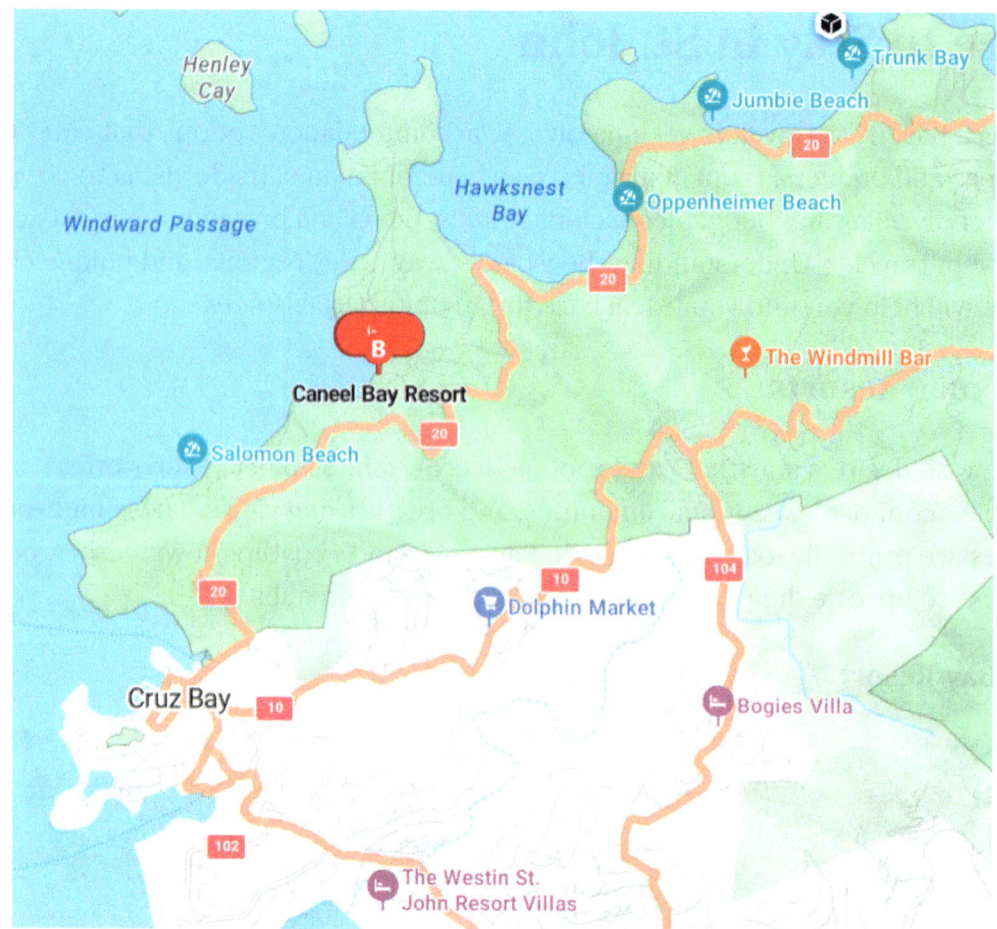

- **Features**: Renowned for its private beaches, gourmet dining options, and eco-friendly design, Caneel Bay Resort is an iconic destination. The resort blends luxury with nature, offering access to seven secluded beaches and world-class snorkeling opportunities.
- **Amenities**: Spa services, guided nature tours, and private water taxis.
- **Pricing**: Rates start at $900 per night for a garden view room; beachfront villas can exceed $2,500 per night.

The Westin St. John Resort Villas

- **Location**: Situated in Great Cruz Bay, a short ferry ride from St. Thomas.

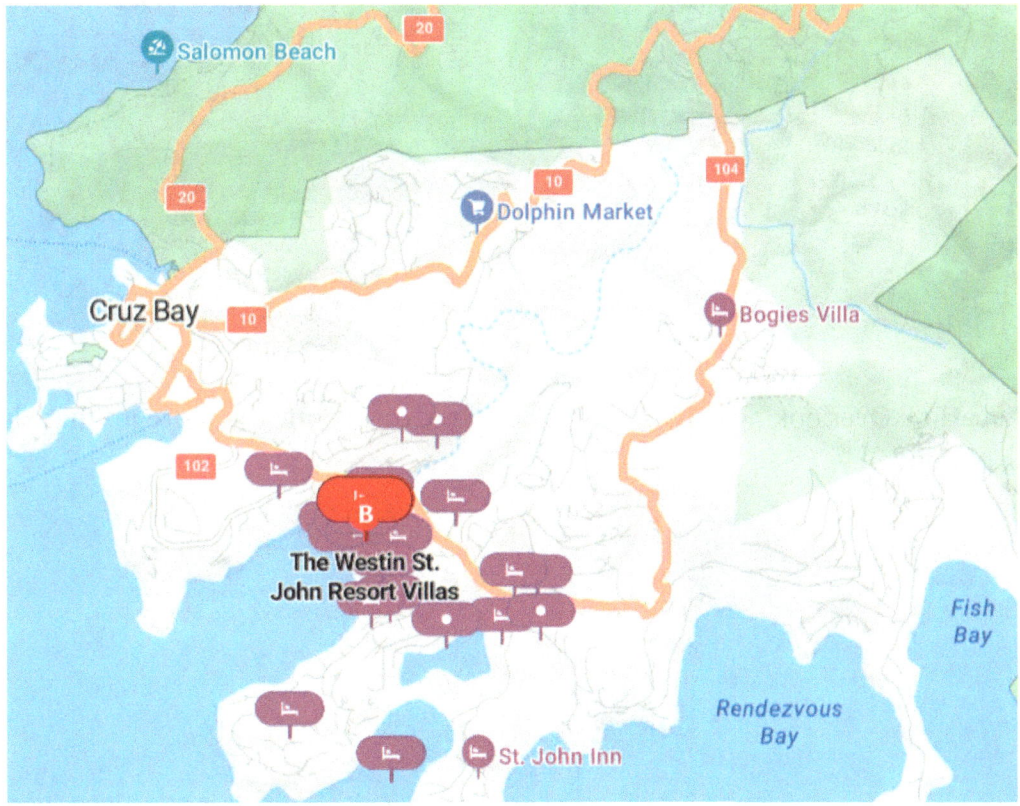

- **Features**: This sprawling resort combines the comfort of private villas with full-service amenities. It's a favorite for families and groups who seek convenience and indulgence.
- **Amenities**: Lagoon-style pool, private beach, water sports rentals, and multiple dining options.
- **Pricing**: Prices range from $600 to $1,800 per night, depending on villa size and season.

Estate Lindholm

- **Location**: Overlooking Cruz Bay, this boutique resort offers a more intimate luxury experience.

- **Features**: A historic property turned into a serene retreat, Estate Lindholm is ideal for couples seeking romance and tranquility.
- **Amenities**: Complimentary breakfast, infinity pool, and stunning views of the bay.
- **Pricing**: Rooms start at $450 per night.

Family-Friendly Accommodations

St. John's family-friendly accommodations focus on creating a welcoming environment for travelers with children. These properties combine convenience with family-oriented amenities to ensure both adults and kids have a memorable stay.

Gallows Point Resort

- **Location**: A prime location in Cruz Bay, within walking distance of restaurants and shops.
- **Features**: Spacious suites equipped with full kitchens make Gallows Point Resort a top choice for families who prefer self-catering options. The lush gardens and snorkeling access add to its charm.
- **Amenities**: Outdoor pool, kid-friendly beach access, and complimentary snorkeling gear.

- **Pricing**: Suites range from $500 to $1,200 per night.

St. John Inn

- **Location**: In Cruz Bay, offering easy access to ferries and local attractions.
- **Features**: This charming inn provides a casual, affordable option for families without compromising on comfort.
- **Amenities**: Complimentary breakfast, outdoor pool, and BBQ facilities.
- **Pricing**: Rates start at $250 per night for standard rooms.

Villa Rentals

- **Location**: Scattered across Coral Bay and Cruz Bay, offering a mix of seclusion and accessibility.
- **Features**: Villas such as Cinnamon Stones or A House of Open Arms provide spacious layouts, private pools, and child-friendly amenities.
- **Pricing**: Family-sized villas typically range from $400 to $1,500 per night, depending on location and amenities.

Budget-Friendly Stays and Rentals

For travelers seeking affordable accommodations without sacrificing the island's charm, St. John offers a range of budget-friendly options. These are often found in Coral Bay or in less-touristy areas, providing a quieter experience.

Cruz Bay Boutique Hotel

- **Location**: Central Cruz Bay, steps from ferry docks and local eateries.

- **Features**: This small hotel combines affordability with convenience, offering clean, modern rooms in the heart of town.
- **Amenities**: Complimentary breakfast, Wi-Fi, and beach gear rentals.
- **Pricing**: Rates start at $200 per night.

Coral Bay Guesthouses

- **Location**: Coral Bay, offering a peaceful escape from the busier Cruz Bay.

- **Features**: Guesthouses such as "The Love Palace" provide simple, cozy accommodations surrounded by natural beauty.
- **Pricing**: Rooms and small cottages start at $150 per night.

Camping at Cinnamon Bay Campground

- **Location**: Within Virgin Islands National Park, directly on Cinnamon Bay Beach.
- **Features**: An excellent option for adventure enthusiasts, this campground offers eco-tents, cottages, and traditional camping spots.
- **Amenities**: Beachfront access, on-site dining, and shared restroom facilities.
- **Pricing**: Rates range from $80 to $200 per night, depending on accommodations.

Locating Your Stay on the Island

St. John's accommodations are concentrated in two main areas, Cruz Bay and Coral Bay, each with distinct atmospheres and advantages. Knowing these differences can help you choose the perfect base for your trip.

Cruz Bay

As the island's main town and transportation hub, Cruz Bay is ideal for those who value convenience and activity. The area is brimming with dining options, bars, and boutique shops. Most luxury resorts, family-friendly accommodations, and budget hotels are within walking distance of the ferry dock.

Best for: Travelers who want to explore Virgin Islands National Park while staying close to restaurants and nightlife.

Coral Bay

Located on the eastern side of the island, Coral Bay offers a more tranquil and rustic vibe. This area is perfect for those who prefer seclusion and proximity to lesser-known hiking trails and beaches. Coral Bay features smaller guesthouses, villas, and camping options.

Best for: Nature lovers and travelers seeking peace and quiet away from the crowds.

Pricing Overview

- **Luxury Resorts**: $450 to $2,500 per night.
- **Family-Friendly Accommodations**: $250 to $1,500 per night.
- **Budget-Friendly Stays**: $80 to $200 per night.

Whether you're seeking opulence, family convenience, or an affordable escape, St. John's diverse accommodations ensure an unforgettable experience. By understanding the island's regions, property types, and amenities, you can tailor your stay to your unique preferences and budget.

Exploring Virgin Islands National Park

Nestled on the breathtaking island of St. John, the Virgin Islands National Park is a treasure trove of natural beauty and cultural heritage. Established in 1956, this park covers over 60% of the island, preserving pristine beaches, lush rainforests, ancient ruins, and vibrant coral reefs. It's a haven for adventurers, nature enthusiasts, and anyone seeking an escape into a world where serenity and splendor collide.

Visiting Virgin Islands National Park is more than just sightseeing; it's an immersive experience that connects you with the island's history, biodiversity, and culture. From hiking through verdant trails to snorkeling in turquoise waters teeming with marine life, the park offers something for everyone. Below is a detailed exploration of this paradise, with essential information on locations, pricing, and how to navigate each part of this iconic landmark.

Overview of the Park

Virgin Islands National Park spans approximately 7,259 acres of land and 5,650 acres of adjacent marine habitats. The park's boundaries encompass an incredible diversity of landscapes, from coastal mangroves and coral reefs to dense tropical forests and historical ruins. The park's headquarters is located in Cruz Bay, making it an easy starting point for visitors to gather information and plan their adventures.

Key Features of the Park:

- **Historical Sites:** The park is home to sugar plantation ruins, such as the Annaberg Plantation, which offer a glimpse into the island's colonial past.
- **Beaches:** Famous stretches of sand like Trunk Bay and Cinnamon Bay are part of the park, drawing visitors with their crystal-clear waters and white sand.
- **Marine Life:** The underwater world here is vibrant, with coral reefs providing a habitat for diverse marine species.
- **Cultural Significance:** Ancient petroglyphs carved by the Taino people can be found along certain trails, adding a layer of mystique to the park.

Entry Fee and Accessibility:

- There is no general entrance fee to the park, but some areas, like Trunk Bay, have a day-use fee of $5 per person.
- Guided tours, including historical and eco-tours, are available at additional costs ranging from $15 to $50.

- The park is accessible via ferry from St. Thomas to Cruz Bay, with round-trip tickets costing around $16 per person.

Top Trails for Hiking

Virgin Islands National Park is a hiker's paradise, boasting over 20 trails that cater to various skill levels. Whether you're a seasoned trekker or a casual explorer, these trails provide an intimate way to experience the park's diverse ecosystems and historical landmarks.

1. Reef Bay Trail

- **Location:** Begins near Centerline Road, about 5 miles east of Cruz Bay.

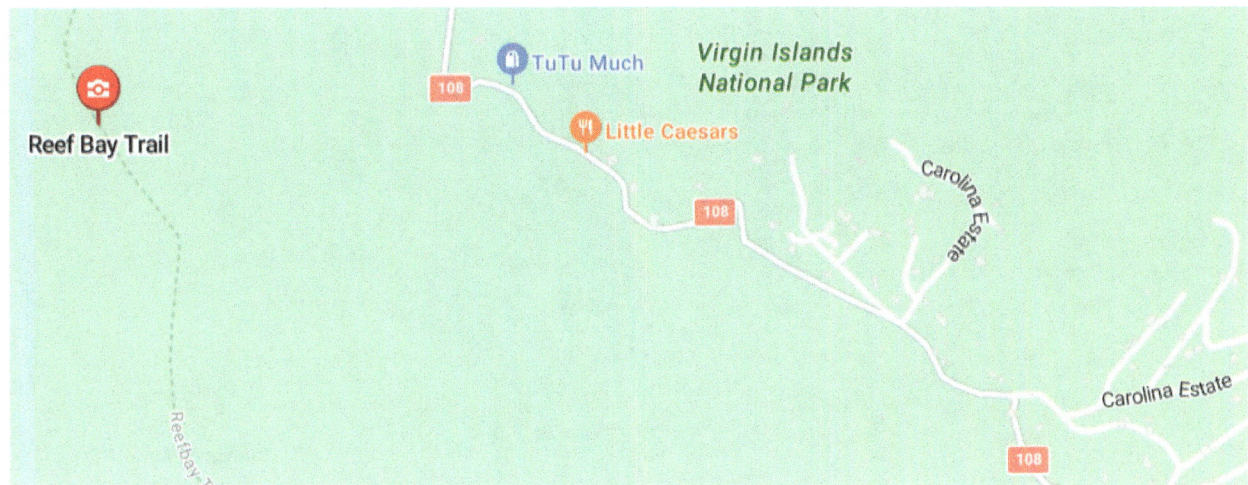

- **Length and Difficulty:** 2.2 miles one way, moderate difficulty.
- **Highlights:**
    - Ancient petroglyphs carved by the Taino people.
    - The ruins of Reef Bay Sugar Factory, a haunting reminder of the island's colonial history.
    - Stunning views of the bay and surrounding forest.
- **Details:** Guided tours are available through the National Park Service, costing $40 per person, including transportation back to the trailhead.

2. Cinnamon Bay Trail

- **Location:** Near Cinnamon Bay Beach, accessible from North Shore Road.

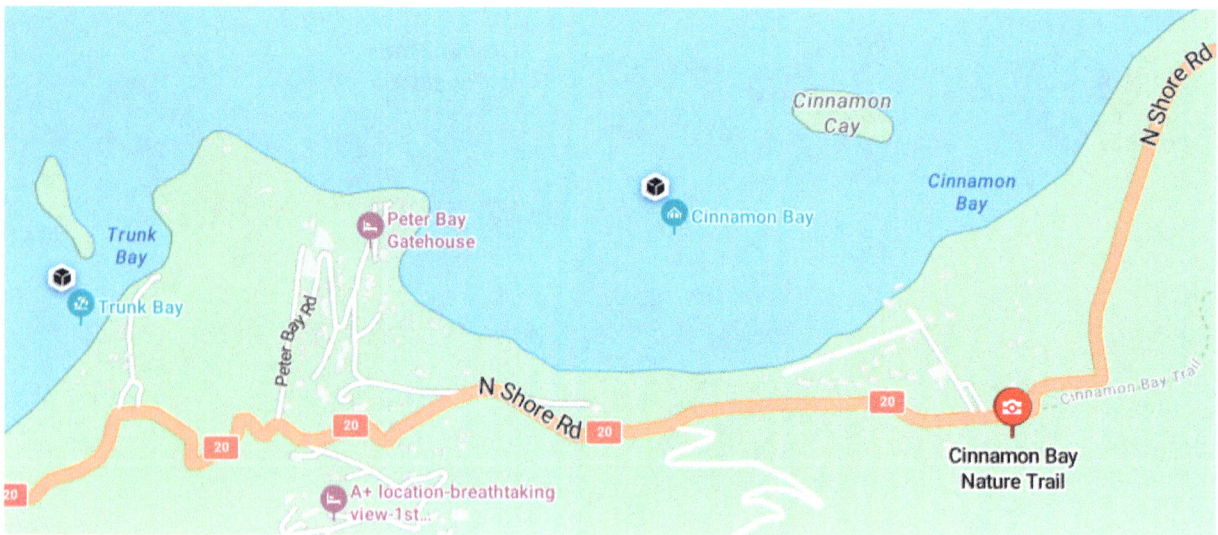

- **Length and Difficulty:** 1 mile one way, easy to moderate difficulty.
- **Highlights:**
  - Ruins of an old Danish plantation.
  - A serene walk through tropical forests.
  - Opportunities for birdwatching along the way.
- **Details:** Free to explore; no permits required.

3. Ram Head Trail

- **Location:** Begins at Salt Pond Bay, on the southeastern tip of the island.

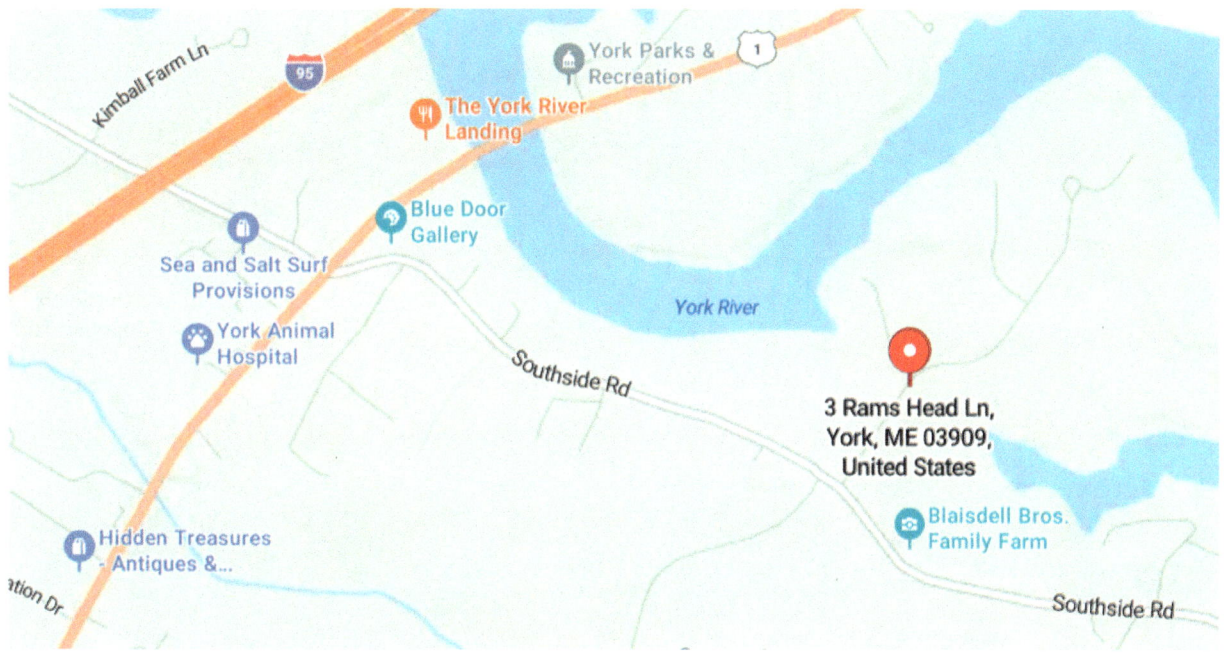

- **Length and Difficulty:** 1 mile one way, moderate difficulty.
- **Highlights:**
  - Sweeping views of the Caribbean Sea and Atlantic Ocean.
  - Unique desert-like terrain with dramatic cliffs.
  - Salt Pond Bay, perfect for a refreshing swim after the hike.
- **Details:** Free to explore, with parking available at the trailhead.

4. Bordeaux Mountain Trail

- **Location:** Starts near Coral Bay, accessible via Bordeaux Mountain Road.

- **Length and Difficulty:** 1.8 miles one way, challenging.
- **Highlights:**
  - Panoramic views from the island's highest point (1,286 feet above sea level).
  - Dense forest vegetation and glimpses of native wildlife.
  - Perfect for adventure seekers looking for a rewarding climb.
- **Details:** Free to access, though the trail may be muddy after rain, so sturdy footwear is recommended.

Wildlife and Nature Experiences

The park's rich biodiversity is one of its most compelling features. From its vibrant coral reefs to its verdant forests, Virgin Islands National Park is home to a stunning array of flora and fauna.

Marine Life

The park's marine habitats are a haven for snorkelers and divers. Coral reefs teem with colorful fish, sea turtles, and rays, providing an underwater spectacle. Popular spots include:

- **Trunk Bay Underwater Snorkel Trail:** Features underwater markers that educate snorkelers about the coral reef ecosystem.
  - **Location:** Trunk Bay, North Shore.

- o **Cost:** Included in the $5 beach fee.
- **Salt Pond Bay:** Known for its calm waters and sightings of nurse sharks and starfish.
  - o **Location:** Southeastern St. John, near Ram Head Trail.
  - o **Cost:** Free to access.

Birdwatching

With over 140 species of birds, St. John is a birdwatcher's delight. Common sightings include:

- **Brown Pelicans:** Often spotted near the coast.
- **Bananaquits:** Bright yellow birds commonly seen in forested areas.
- **Bridled Quail-Doves:** Found in the higher elevations of Bordeaux Mountain.

Tropical Forests

The park's forests are home to unique plant species such as the Bay Rum tree, whose aromatic leaves were once used for essential oil production. Orchids, bromeliads, and giant kapok trees also thrive here, creating a lush environment that is a feast for the senses.

Endangered Species Conservation

The park plays a vital role in protecting endangered species, including:

- **Hawksbill Sea Turtles:** Often seen nesting on park beaches.
- **Green Iguanas:** Frequently spotted in mangrove areas.
- **Coral Reefs:** Conservation efforts focus on combating coral bleaching and restoring reef habitats.

Tips for Exploring the Park

1. **Best Time to Visit:**
   - o The dry season (December to April) is ideal for outdoor activities, with lower humidity and minimal rainfall.
2. **What to Bring:**
   - o Comfortable hiking shoes, sunscreen, insect repellent, and plenty of water are essential for a safe and enjoyable visit.
3. **Guided vs. Self-Guided Tours:**
   - o Opt for guided tours if you're interested in learning about the park's history and ecology. Self-guided explorations are perfect for a flexible schedule.

4. **Safety Precautions:**
   - Be cautious of slippery trails after rain and avoid touching coral reefs while snorkeling to prevent damage to these fragile ecosystems.

Virgin Islands National Park is not just a destination—it's an experience that invites you to connect deeply with nature and history. Each step you take, whether on a sandy beach or a forested trail, reveals a story of preservation and wonder. Whether you're exploring ancient ruins, marveling at coral reefs, or simply soaking in the panoramic views, the park offers endless opportunities to create unforgettable memories.

Beaches of St. John

St. John, often referred to as the crown jewel of the U.S. Virgin Islands, boasts some of the most breathtaking beaches in the world. Its unspoiled sands, crystal-clear waters, and vibrant marine ecosystems create a haven for beachgoers, adventurers, and those seeking solace in nature. Many of these beaches are part of the Virgin Islands National Park, ensuring they remain protected and pristine for generations to come. Whether you seek family fun, romance, or the thrill of underwater exploration, St. John's beaches cater to every type of traveler. Below, we'll delve into three of the island's most iconic beaches: Trunk Bay, Cinnamon Bay, and Honeymoon Beach, each offering a unique experience.

Trunk Bay: The Crown Jewel

Introduction

Trunk Bay is synonymous with St. John's reputation as a tropical paradise. Often ranked among the world's most beautiful beaches, its powdery white sands, turquoise waters, and lush greenery make it a postcard-perfect destination. As part of the Virgin Islands National Park, Trunk Bay's natural beauty is preserved, offering visitors an idyllic escape.

Location and Access

Trunk Bay is situated on the northwestern coast of St. John, approximately 2.5 miles from Cruz Bay. It's easily accessible by car or taxi, with a well-maintained parking lot located near the entrance. For those relying on public transportation, taxis frequently shuttle between Cruz Bay and Trunk Bay, making it convenient for visitors.

Features and Activities

One of Trunk Bay's standout features is its underwater snorkeling trail. This unique attraction allows visitors to explore the vibrant coral reefs and marine life while following underwater plaques that provide educational information about the ecosystem. The trail is ideal for beginners and experienced snorkelers alike, with the shallow waters offering excellent visibility.

Other activities include:

- **Swimming**: The calm waters are perfect for a relaxing dip.
- **Beach Lounging**: The wide expanse of sand provides ample space for sunbathing or simply soaking in the views.
- **Photography**: Trunk Bay's stunning landscapes make it a favorite for photographers and Instagram enthusiasts.

Pricing and Amenities

As part of the Virgin Islands National Park, Trunk Bay charges a small admission fee to help maintain the facilities and preserve the area. Current rates (2025):

- Adults: $5 per person
- Children under 16: Free

Amenities include:

- Restrooms and showers
- Snack bar
- Lifeguards on duty
- Rental kiosks for snorkeling gear and beach chairs

Tips for Visitors

- Arrive early to secure a parking spot and enjoy the beach before it gets crowded.
- Bring reef-safe sunscreen to protect the coral reefs.

- Check the weather and tide conditions to ensure optimal snorkeling visibility.

Cinnamon Bay: Family Fun

Introduction

Cinnamon Bay offers the perfect blend of adventure and relaxation, making it a favorite destination for families. With its expansive shoreline, calm waters, and proximity to hiking trails and historical sites, this beach caters to visitors of all ages. Whether you want to build sandcastles, paddleboard, or explore cultural landmarks, Cinnamon Bay provides a variety of activities.

Location and Access

Located just four miles east of Cruz Bay, Cinnamon Bay is easily reachable by car, taxi, or even bike for the more adventurous. The beach has a designated parking area and is well-signposted from the main road, ensuring easy access for families and groups.

Features and Activities

Cinnamon Bay stands out for its wide array of activities:

- **Hiking**: The nearby Cinnamon Bay Trail leads visitors through lush tropical forests and offers glimpses of historical ruins from the island's sugar plantation era.
- **Water Sports**: Paddleboarding, kayaking, and windsurfing are popular activities here, with rental equipment available on-site.
- **Beach Games**: The expansive shoreline is perfect for volleyball, frisbee, and other family-friendly games.

For those seeking relaxation, the calm and shallow waters make Cinnamon Bay ideal for swimming and wading, especially for families with young children.

Pricing and Amenities

While access to Cinnamon Bay is free, certain activities, such as equipment rentals, come at an additional cost. Approximate rates (2025):

- Kayak rentals: $30/hour
- Paddleboard rentals: $25/hour
- Snorkel gear: $15/day

Amenities include:

- Restrooms and outdoor showers
- A small convenience store for snacks and essentials
- Picnic tables and shaded areas
- Camping facilities for overnight stays

Nearby Attractions

- **Cinnamon Bay Plantation Ruins**: Located just a short walk from the beach, these ruins offer a glimpse into St. John's colonial history.
- **Bordeaux Mountain**: For those up for a challenge, this nearby hike provides panoramic views of the island and surrounding waters.

Tips for Visitors

- Plan a picnic and enjoy the shaded picnic areas with your family.
- Visit during weekdays for a quieter experience, as weekends can get busy.
- If camping, book your spot in advance, as spaces fill quickly during peak seasons.

Honeymoon Beach: A Romantic Getaway

Introduction

Honeymoon Beach is a secluded paradise, perfect for couples seeking a romantic escape. Nestled within the Virgin Islands National Park, this beach is celebrated for its soft sands, crystal-clear waters, and intimate ambiance. Accessible only by a short hike or boat, Honeymoon Beach offers a sense of exclusivity and tranquility that's hard to find elsewhere.

Location and Access

Honeymoon Beach is located on the north shore of St. John, close to Caneel Bay. Visitors can reach the beach via:

- **The Lind Point Trail**: A moderate, 1-mile hike from Cruz Bay that winds through lush forest and offers scenic views of the coastline.
- **Boat Access**: Private charters and water taxis often include Honeymoon Beach in their itineraries.
- **Shuttle Service**: During peak seasons, shuttles operate from Caneel Bay Resort to Honeymoon Beach.

Features and Activities

Honeymoon Beach is renowned for its tranquil atmosphere and array of activities:

- **Snorkeling**: The calm waters and thriving coral reefs make it a hotspot for snorkeling. Sea turtles, rays, and vibrant fish are commonly spotted here.

- **Stand-Up Paddleboarding**: Rent a paddleboard and glide across the serene waters for a unique perspective of the beach.
- **Kayaking**: Explore the coastline or venture to nearby coves by kayak.
- **Relaxation**: With fewer crowds, Honeymoon Beach is ideal for sunbathing, reading, or simply unwinding with your partner.

Pricing and Amenities

Honeymoon Beach does not charge an entry fee, but certain activities and rentals come with costs. Approximate rates (2025):

- Snorkel gear: $20/day
- Paddleboard rentals: $30/hour
- Kayak rentals: $35/hour

Amenities include:

- A beach bar offering drinks and light snacks
- Lounge chair rentals for $15/day
- Restrooms and outdoor showers
- Rental kiosks for water sports equipment

Romantic Highlights

- **Sunset Views**: Stay until the evening to witness breathtaking sunsets that create a magical atmosphere.
- **Private Picnic Spots**: Many areas along the beach offer secluded nooks perfect for a romantic picnic.
- **Couples' Activities**: Sign up for guided kayaking tours designed for two, adding a memorable touch to your visit.

Tips for Visitors

- Wear sturdy shoes if hiking the Lind Point Trail, as the path can be uneven.
- Bring insect repellent for the trail and beach.
- Pack a beach bag with essentials like water, snacks, and sunscreen, as amenities are limited compared to larger beaches.

Outdoor Adventures and Activities in St. John

St. John is an adventure-seeker's paradise, with activities that immerse visitors in its vibrant marine life, lush landscapes, and rich ecological diversity. From exploring underwater worlds to paddling along pristine coastlines, the island offers a variety of experiences tailored to thrill, educate, and inspire. This chapter dives into the top outdoor adventures St. John has to offer, complete with locations, pricing, and detailed guides to help you make the most of your trip.

Snorkeling and Scuba Diving Spots

Explore the underwater wonders of St. John, where crystal-clear waters teem with vibrant coral reefs, colorful fish, and fascinating marine creatures. Whether you're a seasoned diver or a first-time snorkeler, St. John's waters promise unforgettable encounters.

Best Snorkeling Locations

1. **Trunk Bay Underwater Snorkel Trail**
   - **Location**: Trunk Bay, Virgin Islands National Park
   - **Overview**: Trunk Bay's underwater trail is one of the island's most iconic attractions, offering interpretive signs that guide snorkelers through coral gardens teeming with parrotfish, sergeant majors, and sea turtles.
   - **Pricing**: Entry fee of $5 for adults; free for children under 16.
   - **Tips**: Arrive early to avoid crowds and bring reef-safe sunscreen to protect the delicate marine ecosystem.
2. **Honeymoon Beach**
   - **Location**: Caneel Bay
   - **Overview**: Known for its calm, shallow waters, Honeymoon Beach is perfect for beginners and families. The area is home to stingrays, butterflyfish, and starfish.
   - **Pricing**: $49 for a day pass that includes snorkeling gear, kayaks, and paddleboards.
   - **Tips**: Combine your snorkeling adventure with a hike along the Lind Point Trail for breathtaking views.
3. **Waterlemon Cay**
   - **Location**: Leinster Bay
   - **Overview**: A short swim from the shore, Waterlemon Cay is a snorkeler's dream, with thriving coral reefs and a good chance of spotting sea turtles and nurse sharks.

- **Pricing**: Free entry; bring your own gear or rent from Cruz Bay ($20–$30/day).
- **Tips**: Visit early morning or late afternoon to avoid strong currents.

Scuba Diving Adventures

1. **Carvel Rock**
   - **Location**: Off the northeastern tip of the island
   - **Overview**: A dramatic underwater pinnacle, Carvel Rock offers advanced divers the chance to explore caves and tunnels filled with marine life, including lobsters and reef sharks.
   - **Pricing**: Dive tours range from $150 to $200 per person.
   - **Tips**: Strong currents make this site better suited for experienced divers.
2. **Eagle Shoals**
   - **Location**: Southeastern waters of St. John
   - **Overview**: Known for its stunning coral formations and swim-through arches, Eagle Shoals is a bucket-list destination for scuba enthusiasts.
   - **Pricing**: $180 for a two-tank dive, including equipment rental.
   - **Tips**: Book with a reputable operator like **Low Key Watersports** for experienced guides and safety assurances.

Sailing and Kayaking Tours

St. John's calm bays and steady trade winds make it a top destination for sailing and kayaking. These activities allow visitors to discover hidden beaches, dramatic cliffs, and serene coves, all while enjoying the island's turquoise waters.

Sailing Experiences

1. **Sunset Sails**
   - **Location**: Departures from Cruz Bay
   - **Overview**: Watch the sun dip below the horizon aboard a luxury catamaran. Sunset sails often include complimentary drinks and light appetizers, creating a romantic and memorable evening.
   - **Pricing**: $95–$125 per person for a 2-hour tour.
   - **Tips**: Bring a light jacket as it can get breezy on the water during the evening.
2. **Day Charters to Jost Van Dyke**
   - **Location**: Departures from Coral Bay
   - **Overview**: Set sail to the British Virgin Islands, stopping at Jost Van Dyke to explore its famous beach bars and pristine shores. The trip includes snorkeling stops along the way.

- Pricing: $160–$200 per person, including lunch and snorkel gear.
- Tips: Remember your passport for entry into the British Virgin Islands.

3. **Private Yacht Charters**
   - **Location**: Customized itineraries departing from Cruz Bay or Coral Bay
   - **Overview**: For a more exclusive experience, book a private yacht charter to explore St. John's coastline at your own pace.
   - **Pricing**: $800–$1,200 for a half-day charter; $1,500–$2,000 for a full day (up to 6 guests).
   - **Tips**: Coordinate with your captain to visit lesser-known spots like Lovango Cay.

Kayaking Adventures

1. **Mangrove Lagoon Kayak Tour**
   - **Location**: Hurricane Hole, Coral Bay
   - **Overview**: Paddle through the serene mangrove forests of Hurricane Hole, a protected area teeming with juvenile fish, starfish, and sea cucumbers.
   - **Pricing**: $65 per person for a 2-hour guided tour.
   - **Tips**: Wear water shoes for easy entry and exit from the kayak.

2. **Bioluminescent Bay Kayaking**
   - **Location**: Salt Pond Bay (night tours)
   - **Overview**: Experience the magic of bioluminescent plankton illuminating the water with every paddle stroke. This rare natural phenomenon is a highlight for many visitors.
   - **Pricing**: $85 per person for a 2-hour tour.
   - **Tips**: Tours are dependent on moon phases for optimal visibility—book during a new moon for the best experience.

3. **Coastal Kayaking to Rams Head**
   - **Location**: Salt Pond Bay
   - **Overview**: Paddle along the dramatic cliffs of Rams Head, combining kayaking with a short hike to the summit for breathtaking views.
   - **Pricing**: $75 per person for a guided kayak and hike combination.
   - **Tips**: Bring plenty of water and a camera to capture the panoramic views.

Eco-Tours and Sustainable Travel Experiences

St. John's commitment to conservation is evident in its eco-tour offerings, which focus on educating visitors while protecting the island's natural beauty. These tours offer unique opportunities to connect with the environment and learn about the island's flora, fauna, and cultural heritage.

Land-Based Eco-Tours

1. **Reef Bay Trail Guided Hike**
   - **Location**: Virgin Islands National Park
   - **Overview**: Explore the lush forests and historical sites of the Reef Bay Trail, including ancient petroglyphs and sugar mill ruins. The tour concludes with a boat ride back to Cruz Bay.
   - **Pricing**: $40 per person for a guided hike; boat ride is an additional $30.
   - **Tips**: Wear sturdy hiking shoes and bring insect repellent.
2. **Annaberg Plantation Tour**
   - **Location**: Virgin Islands National Park
   - **Overview**: Learn about St. John's history through a tour of the Annaberg Sugar Plantation ruins. Rangers and local guides provide insight into the island's colonial past and its impact on local culture.
   - **Pricing**: Free; donations to the park are encouraged.
   - **Tips**: Visit in the morning to avoid the heat.

Marine Eco-Tours

1. **Coral Restoration Workshops**
   - **Location**: Various locations, including Hawksnest Bay
   - **Overview**: Participate in hands-on coral restoration projects led by marine biologists, learning about reef ecology and contributing to conservation efforts.
   - **Pricing**: $150 per person for a half-day experience.
   - **Tips**: Suitable for all ages; no prior experience required.
2. **Sea Turtle Encounters**
   - **Location**: Maho Bay
   - **Overview**: Observe sea turtles in their natural habitat with guides who ensure minimal disturbance to the animals.
   - **Pricing**: $75 per person for a 2-hour tour.
   - **Tips**: Follow all guidelines to avoid harming the turtles or their environment.

Community-Based Tourism

1. **Cultural Heritage Walks in Coral Bay**
   - **Location**: Coral Bay
   - **Overview**: Join local guides for a walking tour of Coral Bay, exploring its historical landmarks, traditional crafts, and local cuisine.
   - **Pricing**: $50 per person; includes a sampling of local dishes.
   - **Tips**: Support local artisans by purchasing handmade souvenirs.
2. **Volunteer Opportunities**
   - **Location**: Virgin Islands National Park and surrounding areas
   - **Overview**: Visitors can contribute to beach cleanups, trail maintenance, and other conservation efforts through volunteer programs.
   - **Pricing**: Free to participate; donations are welcome.
   - **Tips**: Combine volunteering with sightseeing for a meaningful travel experience.

St. John offers an abundance of outdoor adventures and eco-friendly activities that cater to all interests and skill levels. Whether you're gliding through mangroves, diving into underwater worlds, or hiking through lush trails, the island provides endless opportunities to connect with nature and create unforgettable memories.

Island Culture and Cuisine

Introduction to Island Culture and Cuisine

St. John, the smallest of the U.S. Virgin Islands, is not only a haven for natural beauty but also a vibrant center of cultural traditions and culinary delights. The island's unique blend of African, European, and Caribbean influences is evident in its festivals, music, dance, and food. Visitors to St. John are not just greeted with stunning beaches and lush landscapes but also with a rich cultural tapestry that tells the story of resilience, creativity, and community. The island's culinary scene complements its culture, offering an array of flavors that reflect its diverse heritage. Whether you're attending a local festival or savoring freshly cooked seafood at a beachside eatery, St. John's culture and cuisine promise an unforgettable experience.

Local Festivals and Events

The heart of St. John's culture is its lively festivals, which bring the community together to celebrate history, traditions, and life itself. These events offer visitors an immersive experience into the island's vibrant heritage.

1. St. John Carnival

St. John Carnival, also known as Festival, is the island's most anticipated event of the year. Held annually in June and culminating on July 4th, the Carnival is a colorful display of music, dance, and pageantry.

- **Highlights**: Parades, live music from steel pan bands, and the crowning of Miss St. John.
- **Locations**: Cruz Bay hosts most of the festivities, including the grand parade.
- **Pricing**: Free to attend, but food, drinks, and merchandise are available for purchase. Budget $10–20 for snacks and $20–50 for meals during the festival.

2. Love City Live

This reggae-inspired festival is a celebration of music, love, and community. Typically held in January, it attracts reggae enthusiasts from across the globe.

- **Highlights**: Performances by top reggae artists, beach parties, and food fairs.
- **Locations**: Venues vary, but Cruz Bay and Trunk Bay are popular hotspots.
- **Pricing**: Tickets range from $30–50 for general admission to $100–150 for VIP experiences.

3. St. John Arts Festival

A quieter but equally enriching event, the St. John Arts Festival showcases local art, crafts, and performances every February.

- **Highlights**: Art exhibitions, cultural performances, and traditional music.
- **Locations**: Held in Cruz Bay Park.
- **Pricing**: Free entry, with art pieces available for purchase starting at $20.

4. Full Moon Parties

A more casual and lively affair, full moon parties occur monthly, featuring beach bonfires, music, and dancing under the moonlight.

- **Highlights**: Bonfires, DJ performances, and local food stalls.
- **Locations**: Hansen Bay and Coral Bay.
- **Pricing**: Free entry; food and drinks cost $10–20.

Top Restaurants and Street Food Spots

St. John's culinary scene offers a diverse mix of flavors, from fine dining establishments to humble food trucks. Each spot tells its own story, combining fresh local ingredients with culinary traditions passed down through generations.

1. Fine Dining Restaurants

ZoZo's at the Sugar Mill Located at Caneel Bay, ZoZo's offers an upscale dining experience with breathtaking sunset views.

- **Specialties**: Fresh seafood, handmade pasta, and Italian-inspired dishes.

- **Pricing**: Entrees range from $40–70.
- **Reservations**: Strongly recommended.

Extra Virgin Bistro Nestled in Cruz Bay, this bistro focuses on locally sourced ingredients and inventive cuisine.

- **Specialties**: Lobster risotto and house-made charcuterie.

- **Pricing**: Entrees range from $35–55.
- **Reservations**: Required during peak season.

2. Casual Dining and Cafes

The Longboard A laid-back spot in Cruz Bay, The Longboard is known for its tropical cocktails and healthy yet flavorful dishes.

- **Specialties**: Poke bowls and tacos.

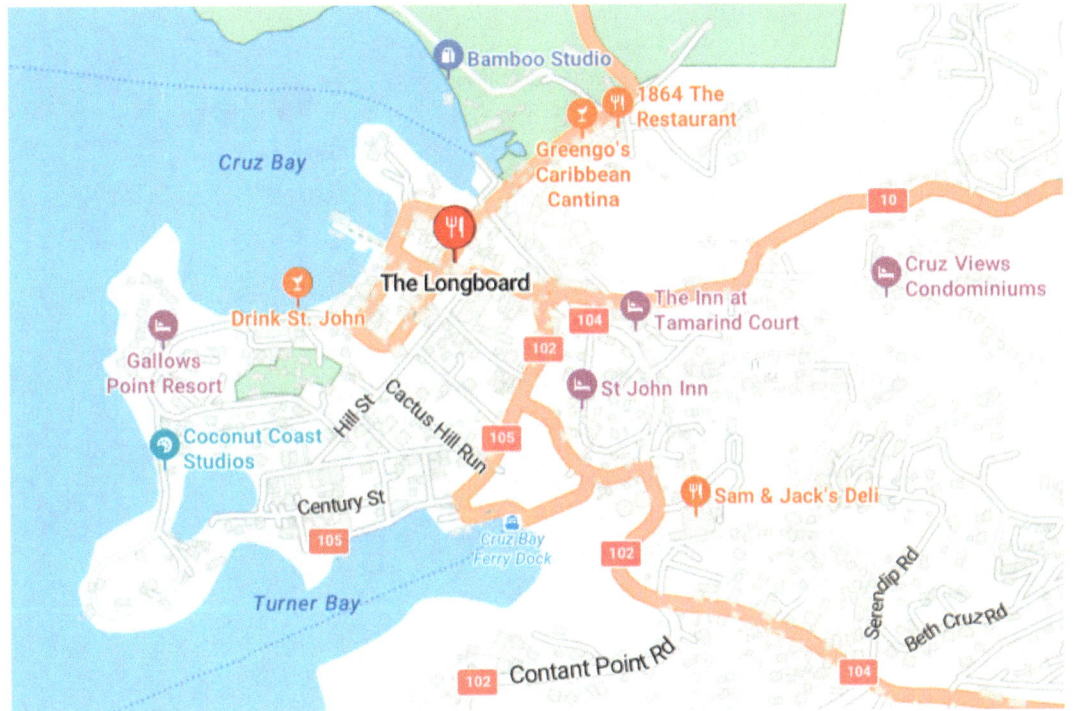

- **Pricing**: $15–30 per dish.

Skinny Legs Located in Coral Bay, Skinny Legs is a beloved local bar and grill.

- **Specialties**: Burgers and cold beers.

- **Pricing**: $12–20 per dish.

3. Street Food and Food Trucks

De' Coal Pot A food truck offering authentic Caribbean dishes with bold flavors.

- **Specialties**: Curry goat, jerk chicken, and plantains.
- **Pricing**: $8–15 per plate.

Grill Master's Food Truck Popular for quick bites and affordable meals.

- **Specialties**: BBQ ribs, grilled fish, and fried plantains.
- **Pricing**: $10–15 per dish.

Traditional Dishes You Must Try

The food of St. John is a delicious reflection of its multicultural history, combining African, European, and Caribbean influences into unique dishes that are both hearty and flavorful.

1. Fungi and Fish

Fungi (pronounced "foon-gee") is a cornmeal-based dish similar to polenta, often served with fish. This staple embodies the essence of traditional island comfort food.

- **Where to Try**: De' Coal Pot or Miss Lucy's Restaurant.
- **Pricing**: $15–25 per plate.

2. Callaloo

This leafy green stew, made with okra, spinach, and sometimes pork or seafood, is a hearty and flavorful dish.

- **Where to Try**: The Longboard and local food trucks.
- **Pricing**: $10–20 per bowl.

3. Johnny Cakes

Fried or baked dough often served as a side or snack, Johnny Cakes are a must-try for visitors.

- **Where to Try**: Available at most local eateries, including food trucks.
- **Pricing**: $2–5 each.

4. Conch Fritters

These fried balls of seasoned conch meat are a popular appetizer across the island.

- **Where to Try**: Skinny Legs and Cruz Bay Café.
- **Pricing**: $10–15 per serving.

5. Saltfish and Dumplings

A traditional breakfast dish featuring salted codfish and soft dumplings, often paired with a side of plantains.

- **Where to Try**: Coral Bay Café and Miss Lucy's.
- **Pricing**: $10–20 per plate.

Shopping and Souvenirs

St. John is a treasure trove of unique shopping experiences, where every purchase tells a story. From handcrafted jewelry inspired by the ocean's beauty to locally-made crafts that preserve the island's cultural heritage, shopping in St. John goes beyond the ordinary. Whether you're exploring bustling artisan markets, tucked-away craft shops, or eco-conscious boutiques, the island offers something for everyone. This guide will take you through the best places to shop, highlight one-of-a-kind souvenirs, and provide tips on how to shop sustainably, ensuring your purchases benefit both you and the local community.

Artisan Markets and Craft Shops

Shopping in St. John isn't just about buying goods; it's an immersive cultural experience. The island's artisan markets and craft shops showcase the creativity and craftsmanship of local artists, giving you the opportunity to take home a piece of the island's soul.

Cruz Bay's Artisan Markets

Cruz Bay, often referred to as the heart of St. John, is home to several artisan markets that buzz with activity. These vibrant markets offer an array of handcrafted goods, from intricate jewelry to vibrant paintings.

- **Mongoose Junction**
  - **Location**: Downtown Cruz Bay, off North Shore Road.
  - **What to Expect**: This charming shopping complex features a blend of high-end boutiques and local artisan stalls. You'll find handcrafted leather goods, pottery, and art pieces that capture the essence of the Caribbean.
  - **Pricing**: Jewelry ranges from $50 to $300; handmade crafts start at $20.
- **The St. John Marketplace**
  - **Location**: Just a short walk from the ferry terminal.
  - **What to Expect**: A bustling market offering everything from locally-produced spices to handmade candles and woven baskets. Vendors are often happy to share the stories behind their creations.
  - **Pricing**: Souvenirs start as low as $10, with premium items like custom artwork priced at $150+.

Coral Bay's Rustic Charm

Coral Bay offers a quieter, more laid-back shopping experience, perfect for discovering hidden gems.

- **Coral Bay Community Market**
  - **Location**: Route 107, Coral Bay.
  - **What to Expect**: This community-focused market features local artisans selling everything from carved wooden figurines to handcrafted soaps. Its tranquil atmosphere makes it ideal for browsing at leisure.
  - **Pricing**: Prices are generally more affordable, with most items ranging between $5 and $50.
- **Pickles in Paradise**
  - **Location**: Just past the Coral Bay intersection.
  - **What to Expect**: A unique mix of a café and artisan shop, offering locally-made goods like painted driftwood signs and island-themed apparel.
  - **Pricing**: Prices start at $15 for smaller items and go up to $100 for larger pieces.

Where to Find Unique Island Souvenirs

Souvenirs are more than keepsakes—they're memories of your journey. St. John offers a wealth of unique items that make for thoughtful gifts or treasured mementos.

Handcrafted Jewelry

Jewelry in St. John often reflects the island's natural beauty, with designs inspired by the ocean, coral reefs, and tropical flora. Many artisans incorporate locally-sourced materials like sea glass, shells, and semi-precious stones.

- **Best Shops**:
  - **Bajo el Sol Gallery** (Cruz Bay): Offers custom-made necklaces and bracelets featuring St. John's iconic turquoise and aquamarine hues. Prices range from $80 to $500.
  - **Bamboula** (Cruz Bay): Known for affordable yet elegant jewelry pieces, with most items priced between $20 and $100.

Locally-Made Spices and Rum

Bring a taste of the Caribbean home with locally-produced spices and rum.

- **St. John Spice**
    - **Location**: Near the ferry dock in Cruz Bay.
    - **What to Buy**: Spice blends like jerk seasoning, Caribbean curry, and hibiscus tea blends. Don't miss their signature hot sauce.
    - **Pricing**: Spice blends start at $7; premium gift sets range from $30 to $50.
- **The Tap Room**
    - **Location**: Mongoose Junction, Cruz Bay.
    - **What to Buy**: Locally-brewed beers and flavored rums, including mango and coconut varieties. Perfect as gifts or for your home bar.
    - **Pricing**: Bottles start at $20.

Artwork and Home Décor

Many local artists use St. John's landscapes as their muse, creating stunning works of art that capture the island's essence.

- **Best Shops**:
    - **Caravan Gallery** (Mongoose Junction): Offers vibrant paintings, sculptures, and handmade ornaments. Prices range from $50 to $500.
    - **Coconut Coast Studios** (Cruz Bay): Specializes in watercolor prints and ceramic pieces inspired by the island's beaches and wildlife. Prices start at $40.

Eco-Friendly Souvenirs

For a sustainable twist, consider items made from recycled or natural materials.

- **Island Green Living EcoStore** (Cruz Bay): Carries eco-friendly products like reusable water bottles, bags made from recycled sails, and bamboo utensils. Prices range from $10 to $50.

Sustainable Shopping Tips

St. John's commitment to sustainability extends to its shopping culture. By making mindful purchases, you can support local communities and protect the island's natural beauty.

1. Choose Locally-Made Products

Opt for items crafted by local artisans rather than mass-produced souvenirs. Not only do these purchases support the community, but they also reduce the carbon footprint associated with imported goods.

2. Avoid Single-Use Plastics

When shopping, bring a reusable bag or opt for stores that use biodegradable packaging. Many shops on the island, like the Island Green Living EcoStore, are leading the way in reducing plastic waste.

3. Invest in Quality Over Quantity

While it's tempting to grab inexpensive trinkets, investing in a high-quality item ensures your souvenir will last and hold sentimental value.

4. Ask About the Story Behind the Product

Many artisans are passionate about their work and are happy to share the inspiration or techniques behind their creations. This connection adds depth to your purchase.

5. Look for Eco-Friendly Certifications

Some products come with certifications indicating sustainable practices, such as recycled materials or fair-trade sourcing. Shops like the Island Green Living EcoStore and Mongoose Junction's boutiques often feature such items.

Day Trips and Nearby Islands

St. John, with its breathtaking scenery and serene atmosphere, is the perfect base for exploring the surrounding islands. Whether you're looking to immerse yourself in local culture, relax on secluded beaches, or dive into thrilling water sports, the nearby islands of St. Thomas, Water Island, and Jost Van Dyke offer unforgettable adventures. In addition, guided tours and private charters ensure you can experience these destinations with ease, making your trip truly seamless.

Excursions to St. Thomas

St. Thomas, just a short ferry ride from St. John, is known as the "gateway to the U.S. Virgin Islands." It's a bustling island that offers a mix of history, shopping, and thrilling activities. Whether you're a history enthusiast, a shopaholic, or someone seeking adrenaline-filled adventures, St. Thomas has something for everyone.

Getting to St. Thomas

- **Ferry Services**: The ferry from Cruz Bay, St. John, to Red Hook, St. Thomas, runs frequently throughout the day.

- ○ **Cost**: $8.15 per person (one way); children's fares are slightly discounted.
- ○ **Travel Time**: Approximately 20 minutes.
- **Private Charter Boats**: Available for those seeking a more exclusive and flexible experience.
  - ○ **Cost**: $400–$700 for a round trip depending on the group size and boat type.

Top Attractions on St. Thomas

1. **Charlotte Amalie**
   - ○ **Overview**: The capital city of the U.S. Virgin Islands is renowned for its Danish colonial architecture and vibrant markets.
   - ○ **Must-See**: The historic 17th-century Fort Christian, the oldest standing structure in the Virgin Islands.
   - ○ **Tip**: Visit the Main Street shopping area for luxury goods, jewelry, and locally crafted souvenirs.

2. **Magens Bay Beach**
   - ○ **Overview**: One of the world's most beautiful beaches, with calm turquoise waters and a mile-long stretch of soft white sand.
   - ○ **Entry Fee**: $5 per person; parking is $2.
   - ○ **Activities**: Kayaking, paddleboarding, and relaxing under the shade of palm trees.

3. **Skyride to Paradise Point**
   - ○ **Overview**: A scenic tram ride that offers panoramic views of Charlotte Amalie and the Caribbean Sea.
   - ○ **Cost**: $25 per person (round trip).
   - ○ **Tip**: Enjoy a signature "Bushwacker" cocktail at the top while taking in the views.

4. **Coral World Ocean Park**
   - ○ **Overview**: A family-friendly attraction featuring marine exhibits, including sea turtles, sharks, and coral reefs.
   - ○ **Entry Fee**: $23.50 for adults, $13 for children.
   - ○ **Activity Highlight**: Interactive experiences like swimming with sea lions or SNUBA diving.

Exploring Water Island and Jost Van Dyke

For those seeking off-the-beaten-path adventures, Water Island and Jost Van Dyke provide tranquil retreats and unique island experiences.

Water Island: A Hidden Gem

Water Island, the smallest of the four main U.S. Virgin Islands, is a quiet haven for those looking to escape the crowds. Its laid-back vibe and natural beauty make it an ideal day-trip destination.

- **Getting There**:
    1. **From St. Thomas**: A short ferry ride from Crown Bay Marina (St. Thomas) takes about 10 minutes.
    2. **Cost**: $6 round trip for adults, $3 for children.
- **Highlights of Water Island**:
    1. **Honeymoon Beach**
        - **Overview**: A pristine, uncrowded beach with calm waters, perfect for swimming and snorkeling.
        - **Facilities**: Chair rentals, food trucks, and a beach bar.
        - **Activity Highlight**: Paddleboard rentals are available for $20/hour.
    2. **Fort Segarra**
        - **Overview**: An unfinished World War II fort with tunnels and stunning views of the surrounding islands.
        - **Cost**: Free entry.
- **Tip**: Bring your own snorkeling gear to explore the underwater world around the island.

Jost Van Dyke: The Island of Parties and Relaxation

Jost Van Dyke, part of the British Virgin Islands, is famous for its festive atmosphere, incredible beach bars, and laid-back charm.

- **Getting There**:
    1. **From St. John**: Reachable via private boat charters or guided tours.
    2. **Cost**: Boat charters range from $700–$1,200 for a full-day trip, depending on the size and amenities of the boat.
- **Entry Requirements**: Since Jost Van Dyke is in the British Virgin Islands, U.S. citizens must carry a passport.
- **Top Spots on Jost Van Dyke**:
    1. **White Bay Beach**

- **Overview**: A postcard-perfect beach with powdery white sand and crystal-clear waters.
- **Highlight**: The Soggy Dollar Bar, where the famous Painkiller cocktail was invented.

2. **Great Harbour**
   - **Overview**: A lively area lined with beach bars and restaurants, including the iconic Foxy's Tamarind Bar.
   - **Tip**: Visit during New Year's Eve for the legendary Old Year's Night celebration.

Guided Tours and Private Boat Charters

For those who want to experience the nearby islands with ease, guided tours and private charters provide a hassle-free and luxurious way to explore the Caribbean.

Guided Tours

Professional tour operators offer a range of options, from snorkeling adventures to cultural explorations. Guided tours are ideal for first-time visitors who want a structured itinerary and expert knowledge.

- **Popular Tour Options**:
  1. **Virgin Islands National Park Snorkeling Tour**
     - **Overview**: A half-day tour exploring the underwater ecosystems around St. John.
     - **Cost**: $75–$100 per person.
     - **Includes**: Snorkeling gear, a guide, and refreshments.
  2. **Historical Island Tour of St. Thomas**
     - **Overview**: A day-long tour covering historical landmarks, markets, and beaches.
     - **Cost**: $60–$85 per person.
     - **Tip**: Book in advance, especially during peak travel seasons.

Private Boat Charters

Private charters offer the ultimate flexibility, allowing you to customize your itinerary and travel in comfort.

- **Cost**:
  1. Half-Day: $500–$800
  2. Full-Day: $1,000–$1,800

3. Includes: Captain, fuel, snorkeling gear, and beverages (varies by operator).

- **Best Private Charter Experiences**:
    1. **Luxury Yacht Tours**
        - **Overview**: Enjoy a day aboard a luxury yacht, complete with catered meals and guided stops at secluded beaches.
        - **Highlight**: Sunset cruises around St. John and neighboring islands.
    2. **Fishing Charters**
        - **Overview**: For angling enthusiasts, private charters can take you to the best fishing spots in the region.
        - **Target Fish**: Mahi-mahi, tuna, and marlin.

Practical Tips for Travelers

Visiting St. John is a dream come true for many, with its untouched landscapes, serene beaches, and vibrant culture. However, to make the most of your trip, careful planning and preparation are essential. This chapter provides detailed insights into safety, health, communication, and packing, ensuring a smooth and enjoyable journey.

Safety and Health Guidelines

St. John is generally a safe destination with a welcoming community and low crime rates, but like any travel destination, staying informed and vigilant is key. Additionally, the island's tropical environment presents unique health considerations that travelers should prepare for.

1. Personal Safety

- **Cruz Bay**: As the main entry point and busiest area, Cruz Bay is generally safe but can get crowded during peak hours. Keep personal belongings close and avoid leaving valuables unattended at beaches or restaurants.
- **Coral Bay**: This quieter area sees less foot traffic and has a relaxed vibe. However, its remoteness means fewer streetlights and emergency facilities, so plan activities during daylight hours.
- **National Park Trails**: Trails like the Reef Bay Trail are well-marked, but solo hiking is discouraged. Always inform someone of your plans and carry essentials like water and a fully charged phone.

2. Emergency Contacts

- **Police Station**: Located in Cruz Bay, it provides immediate assistance. Dial 911 for emergencies.
- **Clinics and Hospitals**: Myrah Keating Smith Community Health Center in Cruz Bay is the primary healthcare facility. Serious cases are often referred to St. Thomas, so travel insurance covering air evacuation is advisable.

3. Health Tips

- **Stay Hydrated**: With high temperatures and humidity, dehydration is common. Carry a reusable water bottle to reduce plastic waste.
- **Insect Protection**: Mosquitoes can carry diseases like dengue fever. Use DEET-based repellents, wear long-sleeved clothing in the evenings, and consider sleeping under a mosquito net.

- **Sun Safety**: The tropical sun can be harsh. Use reef-safe sunscreen to protect both your skin and the marine ecosystem. Hats and UV-protective clothing are highly recommended.

Currency, Language, and Communication

Navigating transactions and communication on St. John is relatively straightforward, but understanding the nuances of local systems will enhance your experience.

1. Currency

- **U.S. Dollar (USD)**: St. John uses the USD, making it convenient for American travelers.
- **ATMs and Credit Cards**:
  - ATMs are available in Cruz Bay, particularly near the ferry dock and shopping areas. Coral Bay has fewer options, so withdraw cash in Cruz Bay if heading there.
  - Credit and debit cards are widely accepted at resorts, restaurants, and larger stores. Smaller vendors and beachside shacks often prefer cash.
- **Tipping**: Standard tipping rates in the U.S. apply. A 15-20% tip is customary in restaurants, while $1-2 per bag is standard for porters and bellhops.

2. Language

- **English**: The official language, spoken fluently by most residents.
- **Creole and Spanish**: You may hear Creole or Spanish spoken among locals, especially in casual settings or smaller communities. Learning basic phrases can foster a friendly rapport.

3. Communication

- **Cell Service**:
  - Major U.S. carriers like AT&T, Verizon, and T-Mobile offer coverage, though signal strength may vary, especially in remote areas like Coral Bay.
  - Consider an international roaming plan if your carrier doesn't include the U.S. Virgin Islands.
- **Wi-Fi Access**:
  - Free Wi-Fi is available in many restaurants, cafes, and resorts. Cruz Bay has better connectivity, while Coral Bay and the national park areas may have limited access.

- **Emergency Communication**: Ensure you have the local emergency numbers saved and a backup power bank for your phone.

Packing Checklist for St. John

Packing for St. John requires a balance of essentials for beach days, hiking adventures, and casual island exploration. Here's a detailed checklist to ensure you're prepared for every aspect of your trip.

1. Clothing Essentials

- **Lightweight and Breathable Clothing**: The tropical climate demands light fabrics like cotton or linen.
- **Swimwear**: Pack multiple swimsuits for beach hopping and water activities.
- **Cover-ups and Sarongs**: Useful for transitioning from beach to restaurant or town.
- **Evening Wear**: Casual dresses or polo shirts are suitable for dining out, especially in Cruz Bay.
- **Hiking Gear**:
  - Moisture-wicking shirts, durable shorts or pants, and a wide-brimmed hat for sun protection.
  - Comfortable hiking shoes or sandals with good grip for trails like Cinnamon Bay Trail or the challenging Reef Bay Trail.

2. Beach and Water Gear

- **Reef-Safe Sunscreen**: Required by law to protect marine life. Available locally, but at a premium price ($15–$20 per bottle).
- **Snorkeling Equipment**: While rentals are available ($10–$15/day), bringing your own ensures quality and comfort.
- **Dry Bag**: Keeps valuables safe during kayaking or snorkeling trips.
- **Beach Towels**: Quick-drying travel towels are space-saving and practical.

3. Health and Safety Items

- **First Aid Kit**: Include basics like band-aids, antiseptic wipes, and pain relievers.
- **Insect Repellent**: Essential for outdoor activities, especially in the evening.
- **Reusable Water Bottle**: Hydration is crucial, and many accommodations offer filtered water refills.

4. Electronics and Accessories

- **Power Bank**: Vital for long hikes or remote excursions.
- **Underwater Camera or GoPro**: Perfect for capturing marine life and underwater adventures.
- **Travel Adapters**: Not necessary for U.S. travelers, as the island uses the same outlets.

5. Documents and Miscellaneous

- **Valid ID or Passport**: While not required for U.S. citizens, it's good to carry a passport for nearby island excursions.
- **Travel Insurance Details**: Include copies of your policy and emergency contact numbers.
- **Printed Maps or Guides**: While cell service may be spotty, printed resources are reliable for navigating trails and beaches.

6. Optional Items

- **Yoga Mat**: Ideal for morning stretches on the beach or resort.
- **Books or E-Readers**: For relaxing downtime.
- **Collapsible Cooler**: Useful for carrying snacks and drinks to remote beaches.

Practical Location Tips

To enhance your packing and preparation, here's a breakdown of specific locations and how packing needs might differ:

- **Cruz Bay**:
  - Pack casual outfits for shopping and dining.
  - Bring extra cash for boutique purchases and tips.
- **Coral Bay**:
  - Prepare for fewer amenities and pack snacks, a cooler, and hiking gear.
- **Virgin Islands National Park**:
  - Hiking gear and water essentials are critical. Ensure you have sturdy shoes and a backpack.
- **Remote Beaches (e.g., Salt Pond Bay)**:
  - Dry bags and snorkeling gear are a must, as rentals may not be available.

By packing strategically and considering location-specific needs, you can focus on enjoying St. John's beauty without the stress of missing essential items.

Seasonal Travel Guide for St. John

St. John is a year-round destination, but the island's seasonal shifts offer distinct experiences that cater to various traveler preferences. Whether you seek tranquil beaches, vibrant festivals, or thrilling outdoor adventures, understanding the nuances of each season will help you plan the perfect getaway. In this chapter, we'll explore the best activities by season, weather patterns to anticipate, and the holiday celebrations and events that define St. John's cultural calendar.

Best Activities by Season

Each season in St. John offers unique opportunities to explore its breathtaking landscapes, vibrant marine life, and cultural experiences. Tailoring your visit to the activities available during specific times of the year can make your trip even more memorable.

Winter (December–February): Peak Travel Season

Why Visit in Winter?
Winter is the most popular season for tourists, as travelers escape cold climates to bask in St. John's warm weather. The island comes alive with bustling beaches, festive events, and a lively atmosphere.

- **Snorkeling and Diving**:
  The clear, calm waters during winter make it an ideal time for snorkeling and diving. Popular spots include Trunk Bay ($5 per person entry fee) and Leinster Bay, where you can explore vibrant coral reefs and swim alongside sea turtles.
- **Hiking in Virgin Islands National Park**:
  Cool breezes and sunny skies create the perfect conditions for hiking trails like the Reef Bay Trail and Ram Head Trail. Guided tours ($50–$75 per person) are available for those who want to delve into the island's history and ecology.
- **Sailing and Sunset Cruises**:
  Charter a private sailboat or join a group cruise from Cruz Bay ($125–$200 per person). Winter sunsets over the Caribbean Sea are truly magical, offering unforgettable views.
- **Whale Watching**:
  Between January and March, humpback whales migrate through the Caribbean. Book a boat tour from Coral Bay ($150 per person) to witness these majestic creatures.

Spring (March–May): The Sweet Spot

Why Visit in Spring?
Spring offers a balance of warm weather, fewer crowds, and competitive pricing, making it a favorite for travelers seeking tranquility without sacrificing adventure.

- **Beach Hopping**:
  Visit quieter beaches like Salt Pond Bay and Maho Bay. Parking at these beaches is free, and you can spend the day enjoying white sands and turquoise waters without the winter crowds.
- **Kayaking and Paddleboarding**:
  Calm seas in spring are perfect for water sports. Rentals are available at Cinnamon Bay Beach, starting at $25 per hour.
- **Cultural Exploration**:
  Spring is an excellent time to explore historical sites like the Annaberg Sugar Plantation Ruins. Entry is free, and guided tours are available for $25 per person.
- **Birdwatching**:
  The Francis Bay Trail is a haven for bird enthusiasts. Look out for brown pelicans, frigatebirds, and bananaquits. Entrance to the trail is free, making it a budget-friendly activity.

Summer (June–August): A Quiet Paradise

Why Visit in Summer?
Summer in St. John sees fewer tourists, making it ideal for those who prefer solitude. While it's hotter, cooling trade winds and frequent ocean dips keep visitors comfortable.

- **Exploring Coral Reefs**:
  Snorkeling at spots like Waterlemon Cay is particularly rewarding in summer, with fewer crowds disturbing the marine life. Equipment rentals are available for $15–$20 per day.
- **Fishing Excursions**:
  Summer is peak season for sport fishing. Charters from Cruz Bay cost $600–$1,200, depending on the duration and group size.
- **Camping Adventures**:
  Embrace the outdoors by staying at Cinnamon Bay Campground. Rates start at $90 per night for eco-tents, offering a unique way to experience the island.
- **Evening Stargazing**:
  Summer skies are clear and perfect for stargazing. Head to the East End for an unobstructed view of the Milky Way.

Fall (September–November): The Off-Season

Why Visit in Fall?
Fall is the least crowded season, offering lower accommodation rates and a serene atmosphere. While it's the height of hurricane season, sunny days still dominate, and travelers can enjoy significant savings.

- **Eco-Tours and Nature Walks**:
  Guided eco-tours of the Virgin Islands National Park ($40–$60 per person) highlight the island's flora and fauna. Fall is also a great time to spot migratory birds.
- **Wellness Retreats**:
  Several resorts, such as The Westin St. John, host yoga and wellness retreats during the fall. Prices range from $250 to $500 per day for inclusive packages.
- **Photography Tours**:
  With fewer tourists, iconic spots like Trunk Bay and the Annaberg Ruins are perfect for capturing stunning photos without interruptions. Professional photography tours cost $100–$200.
- **Island Cuisine Tours**:
  Fall is an excellent time to indulge in local dishes without the crowds. Join a food tour in Cruz Bay ($75 per person) to sample dishes like fungi and Johnnycakes.

Weather Patterns and What to Expect

Understanding the island's weather patterns can help you pack appropriately and plan activities with confidence. While St. John's tropical climate remains warm year-round, each season has its unique characteristics.

Winter (December–February)

- **Temperature**: 77°F–82°F (25°C–28°C).
- **Rainfall**: Minimal, with clear skies dominating.
- **Humidity**: Low, making it the most comfortable season for outdoor activities.
- **What to Pack**: Lightweight clothing, sunscreen, a light jacket for cooler evenings, and water shoes for beach adventures.

Spring (March–May)

- **Temperature**: 78°F–85°F (26°C–29°C).
- **Rainfall**: Slightly higher, but showers are brief.
- **Humidity**: Moderate, with breezy afternoons.

- **What to Pack**: Breathable clothing, a hat, reef-safe sunscreen, and hiking shoes for exploring trails.

Summer (June–August)

- **Temperature**: 80°F–88°F (27°C–31°C).
- **Rainfall**: Increases, but mornings are typically dry.
- **Humidity**: High, but trade winds provide relief.
- **What to Pack**: Quick-dry clothing, insect repellent, a reusable water bottle, and a swimsuit for frequent dips.

Fall (September–November)

- **Temperature**: 79°F–87°F (26°C–30°C).
- **Rainfall**: Highest of the year, with occasional storms.
- **Humidity**: High, contributing to lush greenery.
- **What to Pack**: Waterproof gear, an umbrella, sandals, and a backup power bank for electronics.

Holiday Celebrations and Special Events

St. John's vibrant culture comes alive during its festivals and holidays, providing visitors with opportunities to engage with the island's traditions and local community. These events are scattered throughout the year, offering unique experiences no matter when you visit.

Christmas and New Year's Celebrations (December–January)

The festive season is magical in St. John, with Cruz Bay hosting tree lighting ceremonies, caroling, and parades. Beaches like Trunk Bay feature bonfires and fireworks, creating a tropical twist on traditional holiday celebrations.

- **Key Event**: New Year's Eve in Cruz Bay. Bars and restaurants offer special packages starting at $50, with live music and midnight fireworks.

St. John Carnival (June–July)

One of the most anticipated events, Carnival, showcases the island's vibrant culture through parades, calypso music, and food fairs. Coral Bay hosts a family-friendly version, while Cruz Bay's festivities are livelier.

- **Pricing**: Free to attend, but vendors sell food and drinks ranging from $5 to $20.

- **Highlight**: The Emancipation Day Parade on July 3rd, commemorating the abolition of slavery in 1848.

Thanksgiving Regatta (November)

This two-day sailing event in Coral Bay is a favorite among locals and visitors alike. The regatta includes competitive races, live music, and delicious food.

- **Pricing**: Free for spectators; entry fees for sailors start at $100 per boat.
- **Best Spot**: Coral Bay harbor offers excellent views of the race.

Full Moon Parties (Monthly)

Held at various locations, including Maho Crossroads, full moon parties feature live music, fire dancers, and local cuisine. These gatherings are a great way to experience St. John's nightlife and community spirit.

- **Pricing**: Entry is free; food and drinks cost $10–$25.
- **Best Time**: Arrive early to secure a spot and enjoy the sunset before the party begins.

St. John's seasonal charm ensures there's never a wrong time to visit. By aligning your travel plans with the activities, weather, and cultural events that appeal most to you, your journey to this Caribbean gem will be nothing short of extraordinary.

Sustainability and Conservation

St. John, with its unspoiled natural beauty and vibrant ecosystems, has long been a model for sustainable tourism and conservation. Nearly two-thirds of the island is protected by the Virgin Islands National Park, a testament to the island's commitment to preserving its unique landscapes and wildlife. From protecting coral reefs to promoting eco-friendly travel, St. John offers visitors a chance to experience its wonders responsibly. This chapter provides a comprehensive guide to traveling sustainably on the island, supporting local communities, and getting involved in conservation efforts.

How to Travel Responsibly in St. John

Traveling responsibly in St. John starts with an awareness of the island's delicate ecosystems and the impact of tourism. Visitors can take simple steps to reduce their footprint while enjoying everything this tropical paradise has to offer.

1. Choose Eco-Friendly Accommodations

Many hotels, resorts, and vacation rentals on St. John prioritize sustainability. These properties adopt energy-efficient practices, minimize waste, and support local communities.

- **Caneel Bay Resort**: Located within the Virgin Islands National Park, this eco-conscious resort integrates sustainable practices into its operations. Guests can enjoy luxurious accommodations while knowing they are supporting conservation efforts. Prices range from $450–$1,000 per night.
- **Estate Lindholm**: A charming boutique hotel in Cruz Bay that incorporates solar energy and water conservation systems. Rates start at $300 per night.
- **Eco-Tents at Cinnamon Bay Campground**: Perfect for nature enthusiasts, these tents offer a unique experience close to the beach while promoting minimal environmental impact. Prices range from $80–$150 per night.

2. Reduce Plastic Waste

Plastic pollution poses a significant threat to St. John's marine life and beaches. Visitors can help by:

- Carrying reusable water bottles and shopping bags.
- Avoiding single-use plastics and opting for biodegradable products.
- Participating in beach clean-up events organized by local groups like Friends of the Virgin Islands National Park.

3. Respect Coral Reefs and Marine Life

St. John's coral reefs are among the island's most valuable natural assets, providing habitat for diverse marine species. To protect these ecosystems:

- Avoid using sunscreen with harmful chemicals like oxybenzone and octinoxate. Opt for reef-safe sunscreen, available at local shops in Cruz Bay for around $15–$20.
- Refrain from touching or standing on corals while snorkeling or diving.
- Choose eco-certified tour operators for water-based activities.

4. Minimize Carbon Footprint

Walking, cycling, and using public transportation are excellent ways to reduce carbon emissions while exploring St. John. The island is compact and walkable, with trails and scenic paths connecting many attractions. Additionally, electric vehicle rentals are available at companies like Sun Plugged Car Rentals, with prices starting at $60 per day.

Supporting Local Communities and Businesses

St. John's charm lies not only in its natural beauty but also in its vibrant local culture. By supporting local businesses and artisans, visitors can directly contribute to the island's economy and help preserve its traditions.

1. Shop at Local Markets

Cruz Bay is home to several artisan markets where visitors can purchase handmade goods, souvenirs, and locally produced items:

- **The Bajo el Sol Gallery**: Located in Mongoose Junction, this gallery features art, pottery, and jewelry created by local artists. Prices range from $30–$500.
- **Caribbean Craft Market**: A collection of stalls offering handcrafted items like woven baskets, seashell jewelry, and coconut carvings. Prices start as low as $10.

2. Dine at Locally Owned Restaurants

Savor the flavors of St. John by dining at restaurants that use locally sourced ingredients:

- **The Longboard**: A casual spot in Cruz Bay serving Caribbean-inspired dishes with a sustainable twist. Popular items include fresh seafood tacos and tropical cocktails. Meals typically cost $15–$30.
- **Miss Lucy's**: Located in Coral Bay, this iconic eatery offers traditional Virgin Islands dishes like conch fritters and johnnycakes. Expect to spend $20–$40 per meal.

- **St. John Provisions**: A small café known for its organic coffee and baked goods, with prices starting at $5.

3. Support Local Tours and Activities

Choose tour operators and guides that prioritize sustainability and employ local residents:

- **Virgin Islands EcoTours**: Offers kayaking, snorkeling, and hiking tours with a focus on environmental education. Prices range from $50–$100 per person.
- **Cultural Walking Tours**: Led by local historians, these tours explore the island's heritage and lesser-known landmarks. Prices start at $25 per person.

Volunteer Opportunities and Conservation Efforts

For travelers seeking a deeper connection with St. John, volunteering offers a meaningful way to give back to the island. From beach clean-ups to wildlife monitoring, there are plenty of opportunities to contribute to ongoing conservation efforts.

1. Join Beach Clean-Ups

Local organizations frequently host beach clean-up events to combat plastic pollution and keep the island's shores pristine.

- **Friends of the Virgin Islands National Park**: This nonprofit organizes regular clean-ups at popular beaches like Trunk Bay and Hawksnest Beach. Visitors can sign up on their website or inquire at their office in Cruz Bay.

2. Participate in Wildlife Conservation Programs

Protecting St. John's biodiversity is a key priority. Visitors can volunteer for programs that focus on monitoring and safeguarding local species:

- **Sea Turtle Nest Monitoring**: Assist researchers during nesting season (May–November) by monitoring beaches for nesting activity. This program is run by the National Park Service, and participation is free, though donations are encouraged.
- **Coral Reef Restoration**: Join efforts to restore damaged reefs by helping with coral planting initiatives. Programs are available through organizations like the Coral Bay Community Council, with suggested donations of $50–$100.

3. Volunteer at the Virgin Islands National Park

The park offers a variety of volunteer opportunities, from trail maintenance to historical preservation:

- **Trail Maintenance Crews**: Help clear and maintain hiking trails like the Reef Bay Trail or the Lind Point Trail. Tools and training are provided by the park staff.
- **Historical Site Preservation**: Assist in preserving landmarks such as the Annaberg Plantation ruins by participating in restoration projects.

4. Support Educational Outreach Programs

Visitors can contribute to local education by volunteering at schools or community centers. Programs often include teaching environmental stewardship or helping with literacy initiatives.

Hidden Gems of St. John

St. John, a slice of Caribbean paradise, is renowned for its pristine beaches and lush landscapes, but its most captivating treasures often lie beyond the usual tourist paths. This chapter unveils the hidden gems of St. John, inviting travelers to discover off-the-beaten-path beaches, underrated trails, and attractions that remain largely untouched by crowds. With detailed insights, practical tips, and pricing information, you'll have everything you need to explore St. John like a local.

Off-the-Beaten-Path Beaches

Intro: While Trunk Bay and Cinnamon Bay draw much of the spotlight, St. John's coastline is dotted with secluded beaches that offer tranquility and untouched beauty. These lesser-known spots are perfect for travelers seeking privacy, unique landscapes, and pristine snorkeling experiences.

1. **Hansen Bay Beach**

- ○ **Location**: East End of St. John, approximately 30 minutes from Cruz Bay.
- ○ **Why It's Special**: Hansen Bay offers calm, crystal-clear waters and an intimate vibe, perfect for snorkeling and paddleboarding. The beach is

privately owned but accessible for a small donation, ensuring a serene and uncrowded experience.

- o **Activities**: Rent paddleboards or kayaks from the locals who manage the beach. Snorkel along the rocky shoreline to spot vibrant coral reefs and marine life, including rays and turtles.
- o **Pricing**: Suggested donation of $5-$10 per person. Paddleboard rentals start at $20/hour.
- o **Tips**: Arrive early to secure a shady spot, and bring cash for donations and rentals.

2. **Salt Pond Bay**

- o **Location**: Near Coral Bay on the southeastern side of the island.
- o **Why It's Special**: Known for its unique salt ponds, this beach combines calm waters with hiking opportunities. It's a fantastic spot for families or nature enthusiasts looking to explore beyond the sand.
- o **Activities**: Snorkel to discover colorful fish and coral reefs, or hike the nearby Ram Head Trail for breathtaking views. The salt pond area is also home to unique flora and fauna.
- o **Pricing**: Free entry; donations to the National Park are encouraged.
- o **Tips**: Pack sturdy shoes for hiking and plenty of water, as the area can get hot during midday.

3. **Lameshur Bay Beaches**

- ○ **Location**: South side of the island, accessible via a rugged dirt road from Coral Bay.
- ○ **Why It's Special**: This pair of beaches, Little Lameshur and Great Lameshur, offers a secluded escape with some of the best snorkeling on the island. The surrounding area is steeped in history, with remnants of Danish plantation ruins nearby.
- ○ **Activities**: Snorkel along the rocky shoreline to see schools of fish and coral gardens, or relax under the shade of sea grape trees.
- ○ **Pricing**: Free, but a high-clearance vehicle is recommended for access.
- ○ **Tips**: Bring your own gear and snacks, as there are no facilities in the area.

Underrated Trails and Attractions

Intro: Beyond the well-trodden paths of Virgin Islands National Park, St. John offers a treasure trove of lesser-known trails and attractions. These spots are perfect for adventurers looking to uncover the island's hidden history, unique landscapes, and cultural landmarks.

1. **Reef Bay Trail Petroglyphs**
   - **Location**: Accessible via the Reef Bay Trail in Virgin Islands National Park.
   - **Why It's Special**: The petroglyphs, created by the Taino people, are one of St. John's most fascinating historical artifacts. Nestled near a freshwater pool, these carvings depict ancient symbols that tell stories of the island's Indigenous heritage.
   - **Hike Details**: The trail is moderately challenging, descending approximately 2.2 miles through lush forest to the petroglyphs.
   - **Pricing**: Free entry; guided tours with the National Park Service are $40/person.
   - **Tips**: Wear sturdy hiking shoes, and bring plenty of water and bug spray. Consider taking a guided tour to learn more about the site's history.

2. **America Hill Ruins**
   - **Location**: Near Cinnamon Bay, a short hike off the Cinnamon Bay Trail.
   - **Why It's Special**: These ruins offer a glimpse into St. John's colonial past, with the remains of a plantation house perched on a hill with panoramic views of the island and nearby cays.
   - **Hike Details**: The hike to the ruins is approximately 0.3 miles, with some steep sections.
   - **Pricing**: Free.
   - **Tips**: Visit in the morning or late afternoon for cooler temperatures, and take your time exploring the ruins and enjoying the views.

3. **Haulover Bay**
   - **Location**: East End of St. John, near Hansen Bay.
   - **Why It's Special**: Haulover Bay is a hidden snorkeling paradise, offering stunning underwater landscapes with fewer crowds. The beach is divided into two sides, Haulover North and Haulover South, each with unique features.
   - **Activities**: Snorkeling is the main draw, with vibrant coral reefs and abundant marine life. The northern side is rockier, while the southern side offers calmer waters.
   - **Pricing**: Free.

- Tips: Bring your snorkeling gear and water shoes for navigating the rocky shoreline.

Insider Tips from Locals

Intro: To truly experience St. John like a seasoned traveler, tap into the wisdom of the locals. From dining recommendations to secret viewpoints, these insider tips will help you uncover the island's authentic charm.

1. **Local Dining Favorites**
   - **Skinny Legs**: A Coral Bay institution, this laid-back burger joint is loved for its casual vibe and mouthwatering food.
     - **Pricing**: Burgers start at $12; cash only.
   - **Sam & Jack's Deli**: Located in Cruz Bay, this spot is known for its gourmet sandwiches and picnic-friendly meals.
     - **Pricing**: Sandwiches range from $10-$15.
   - **Tips**: Ask about daily specials and grab a meal to go for a beach picnic.
2. **Best Sunset Spots**
   - **Peace Hill**: This short hike leads to stunning sunset views overlooking Hawksnest Bay and Jost Van Dyke.
   - **Maho Bay**: Arrive early to secure a spot on the sand and watch the sun dip below the horizon.
3. **Secret Viewpoints**
   - **Ram Head Trail Overlook**: While many stop at the trail's endpoint, locals suggest venturing slightly further for a secluded vantage point with sweeping ocean views.
   - **Gift Hill**: Accessible by car, this spot offers panoramic views of St. Thomas and the British Virgin Islands.
4. **Local Markets and Shops**
   - **Cruz Bay Farmers Market**: Held weekly, this market features fresh produce, handmade crafts, and local delicacies.
   - **Caravan Gallery**: A treasure trove of unique jewelry and gifts made by local artisans.
5. **Timing Your Visit**
   - Visit popular spots early in the morning or late in the afternoon to avoid crowds and enjoy cooler temperatures.
   - Plan your trip during off-peak months (April-June) for better deals and fewer tourists.

Practical Tips for Exploring Hidden Gems

- **Transportation**: A rental car is essential for reaching remote areas. Opt for a Jeep or high-clearance vehicle for rugged roads.
- **Packing Essentials**: Bring water, snacks, sunscreen, and bug spray, especially for hikes and less-developed areas.
- **Local Etiquette**: Respect private property, and always ask permission before entering areas marked as private.
- **Eco-Conscious Travel**: Leave no trace by packing out your trash and avoiding the use of single-use plastics.

By venturing beyond the well-known attractions, you'll uncover the true essence of St. John—a blend of natural beauty, rich history, and warm hospitality that leaves an indelible mark on every visitor.

Departure and Farewell

Leaving St. John can be bittersweet. As your time on the island comes to an end, it's essential to make the most of your final hours, ensuring your departure is smooth and memorable. From savoring last-minute experiences to practical travel tips, this guide will help you bid farewell to St. John in the most meaningful way possible. Let's delve into the best ways to wrap up your visit, navigate your journey home, and reflect on the unforgettable memories made during your stay.

Making the Most of Your Last Day

Your final day in St. John presents the perfect opportunity to soak in the island's beauty one last time. Whether it's a leisurely beach morning, a scenic hike, or indulging in local cuisine, ensure you leave the island with cherished memories.

1. **Morning Serenity at Trunk Bay**
   - **Location**: North Shore Road, Virgin Islands National Park
   - **Pricing**: $5 entry fee per person (free for children under 16)
   - **Why Visit**: Known for its crystal-clear waters and iconic underwater snorkeling trail, Trunk Bay is a serene spot to begin your day. Arrive early to avoid crowds and enjoy a peaceful swim or snorkel as the sun rises.
2. **Final Hike on the Lind Point Trail**
   - **Location**: Trailhead near Cruz Bay Visitor Center
   - **Pricing**: Free (no entrance fee required)
   - **Why Visit**: This moderate 2-mile round-trip hike offers stunning views of Cruz Bay and Honeymoon Beach. It's an ideal way to connect with nature and capture final panoramic shots of the island.
3. **Lunch at The Longboard**
   - **Location**: 7150 Cruz Bay, St. John
   - **Pricing**: $15–$30 per dish
   - **Why Visit**: This Caribbean-inspired restaurant serves fresh seafood and vibrant cocktails. Opt for their poke bowls or ceviche paired with a refreshing frozen cocktail.
4. **Beachside Relaxation at Cinnamon Bay**
   - **Location**: North Shore, Virgin Islands National Park
   - **Pricing**: Free entry; $5–$10 for lounge chair rentals
   - **Why Visit**: Spend your afternoon unwinding on this tranquil beach, with its soft white sands and gentle waves. The on-site amenities, including showers and a snack bar, make it a comfortable spot for your last hours on the island.

Tips for Smooth Departures

Leaving St. John requires a bit of planning, especially if you're coordinating ferries, flights, and transfers. To ensure your journey home is hassle-free, follow these tips:

1. **Plan Your Ferry Transfer**
   - **Ferry Options**: Ferries from Cruz Bay to St. Thomas operate daily, with the last ferry typically departing around 8:00 PM. Schedules can vary, so check the latest timetable in advance.
   - **Pricing**: $8.15 per adult, $1 per child under 12 (one-way).
   - **Tip**: Arrive at the ferry dock at least 20 minutes before departure to secure your spot.

2. **Coordinate with Your Hotel or Rental Host**
   - Many accommodations offer late checkout options or luggage storage for a small fee. If available, take advantage of this service to enjoy your last day without worrying about your belongings.

3. **Book a Taxi in Advance**
   - **Taxi Service**: St. John Taxi Association offers reliable transport to the ferry dock.
   - **Pricing**: Approximately $6–$15 per person, depending on the distance.
   - **Tip**: Reserve your taxi the night before to ensure timely arrival at the ferry.

4. **Prepare for Customs and Security**
   - As St. John is part of the U.S. Virgin Islands, U.S. citizens don't require a passport, but you'll still need to clear customs when leaving the territory.
   - **Tip**: Have valid photo ID and proof of return travel ready.

5. **Pack Smartly**
   - **Luggage Restrictions**: Be mindful of weight limits and restrictions for ferries and connecting flights. Pack your souvenirs carefully to prevent damage.

6. **Stay Connected**
   - Download any travel apps you may need for ferry schedules, flight updates, or emergency contacts. Reliable apps include USVI *Travel* and *Ferry Schedules USVI*.

Reflecting on Your St. John Adventure

As you prepare to leave, take time to reflect on the unique experiences that made your trip special. Whether it's the serene beaches, the breathtaking hikes, or the warm hospitality of the locals, every moment spent on St. John adds a layer of richness to your memories.

1. **Create a Travel Journal**
   - Before you leave, jot down your favorite moments, such as the first time you glimpsed Trunk Bay or the delicious meals you enjoyed. Add photos, ticket stubs, or small mementos to make it a keepsake.
2. **Capture a Last Photo**
   - Stop by the Cruz Bay waterfront or a scenic overlook like Peace Hill to take a final photograph of the island. These images will serve as a lasting reminder of your journey.
3. **Express Gratitude**
   - Thank the locals who made your stay memorable, from your tour guides to restaurant staff. A simple gesture of appreciation can leave a positive impression and strengthen the connection between visitors and the community.
4. **Plan Your Return**
   - As you reflect, you may find yourself already dreaming of your next visit. St. John has a way of leaving a lasting impression, making it a destination many travelers return to time and again.

Sample Itinerary for Your Last Day in St. John

- **Morning**: Start your day at Trunk Bay with a sunrise swim and snorkel.
- **Mid-Morning**: Take a short hike on the Lind Point Trail to enjoy panoramic views of Cruz Bay.
- **Lunch**: Dine at The Longboard for fresh, local cuisine.
- **Afternoon**: Relax at Cinnamon Bay, soaking up the sun and savoring the tranquility.
- **Evening**: Board your ferry to St. Thomas, bidding farewell to the island as the sun sets.

Closing Thoughts

As you leave St. John, you're not just saying goodbye to an island but to an experience filled with natural beauty, cultural richness, and moments of pure joy. The memories you've made here will stay with you long after your departure, a testament to the magic of this Caribbean gem. While the farewell may be tinged with sadness, it also comes with the promise of a return, because once you've experienced St. John, it's impossible not to dream of coming back.

Resources and Contacts

St. John's serene beauty and relaxed atmosphere make it an inviting destination, but being well-prepared ensures your visit is smooth and enjoyable. Whether you're exploring the Virgin Islands National Park, navigating the lively streets of Cruz Bay, or relaxing in the secluded corners of Coral Bay, having access to reliable resources and contacts can make all the difference. This chapter dives into essential emergency numbers, traveler-friendly apps, and curated reading materials to help you make the most of your trip.

Emergency Numbers and Useful Contacts

Emergencies can occur even in paradise, and knowing whom to contact can be a lifesaver. Whether you need medical assistance, help with transportation, or general information, these resources are crucial during your stay.

Emergency Services on St. John

The U.S. Virgin Islands have well-established emergency response systems, but it's worth noting that St. John's smaller size may mean a slight delay in services compared to larger islands. For immediate assistance, use the following numbers:

- **Police Department (Cruz Bay Station)**: +1 (340) 693-8880
- **Emergency Dispatch (Police, Fire, and Medical)**: 911
- **Myrah Keating Smith Community Health Center** (24-hour medical assistance): +1 (340) 693-8900
- **Fire Department (Cruz Bay Fire Station)**: +1 (340) 776-6333
- **Coast Guard Emergency**: +1 (340) 776-3497

Tourist Assistance

If you encounter issues related to lost property, safety concerns, or require travel-related guidance, these contacts will be helpful:

- **U.S. Virgin Islands Department of Tourism (St. John Office)**: +1 (340) 774-8784
- **National Park Visitor Center (Cruz Bay)**: +1 (340) 776-6201
- **St. John Rescue (Volunteer Emergency Response Organization)**: +1 (340) 693-7377

Key Locations for Emergency Services

- **Myrah Keating Smith Community Health Center**: Located 3 miles from Cruz Bay, on Centerline Road, this is the primary healthcare facility on the island. Services include urgent care, minor trauma treatment, and pharmacy access.
  - **Hours**: Open 24/7 for emergencies
  - **Pricing**: Costs vary depending on services; ensure you have travel insurance to cover medical expenses.
- **Cruz Bay Fire Station**: Located near the ferry dock in Cruz Bay, this is the island's main fire department. It's easily accessible for most visitors staying in Cruz Bay or nearby.

Recommended Apps for Travelers

Smartphones have become indispensable for modern travel. The right apps can help you navigate the island, find the best spots, and stay informed about local events.

Navigation and Transportation Apps

- **Google Maps**: Reliable for general navigation around St. John, including driving directions for rental vehicles and walking paths to major attractions.
  - **Tips**: Download offline maps before arrival for uninterrupted use in areas with poor connectivity.
- **VI Now**: This comprehensive app provides ferry schedules, local news, and recommendations for restaurants, activities, and events across the Virgin Islands.
  - **Available on**: iOS and Android
  - **Cost**: Free

Outdoor Adventure Apps

- **AllTrails**: Ideal for hikers exploring the trails of Virgin Islands National Park. The app offers detailed trail maps, difficulty ratings, and user reviews.
  - **Features**: GPS tracking and offline map downloads.
  - **Cost**: Free version available; premium subscriptions start at $29.99/year.
- **Snorkel Report**: Real-time updates on snorkeling conditions, including water clarity and marine life sightings.
  - **Cost**: Free with optional donations to support marine conservation.

Communication and Emergency Apps

- **WhatsApp**: Essential for international travelers to stay connected with family, friends, and local contacts using Wi-Fi.
  - **Cost**: Free
- **Red Cross First Aid App**: Offers step-by-step guidance for managing medical emergencies, making it a valuable tool for travelers in remote areas of the island.
  - **Cost**: Free

Additional Reading and Travel Resources

Educating yourself about St. John's history, culture, and natural environment can enrich your visit and create a deeper connection to the island. Here's a curated list of books, websites, and guides to inspire and inform your trip.

Books About St. John

- **"St. John Off the Beaten Track" by Gerald Singer**
  - This guidebook is a must-have for adventurers. It features detailed descriptions of lesser-known hiking trails, beaches, and historical sites.
  - **Available at**: Local bookstores in Cruz Bay and online retailers.
  - **Price**: Approximately $19.95
- **"Island Home: Why the Virgin Islands Will Always Be Home" by Chuck Ball**
  - A heartwarming memoir that explores life in the Virgin Islands, with vivid descriptions of St. John's landscapes and culture.
  - **Price**: Around $14.99
- **"National Geographic's Guide to National Parks of the United States"**
  - This comprehensive guide includes an informative section on Virgin Islands National Park, with stunning photography and practical tips.
  - **Price**: Approximately $29.95

Online Resources

- **Virgin Islands National Park Official Website**:
  - Features trail maps, event calendars, and information on park regulations.
  - **Website**: www.nps.gov/viis
- **USVI Department of Tourism**:
  - The go-to resource for travel planning, offering information on accommodations, transportation, and local events.
  - **Website**: www.visitusvi.com

- **St. John Tradewinds News**:
    - A local online newspaper providing updates on island news, events, and community activities.
    - **Website**: www.stjohntradewindsnews.com

Where to Access These Resources

- **Cruz Bay Visitor Center**: A hub for tourist information, offering free maps, brochures, and advice from knowledgeable staff.
    - **Hours**: 8:00 AM – 4:30 PM (Monday to Friday)
    - **Location**: Near the Cruz Bay ferry dock.
    - **Cost**: Free
- **Coral Bay Information Kiosk**: A smaller but equally resourceful spot, ideal for travelers exploring the eastern side of the island.

Practical Tips for Using Resources and Contacts

1. **Save Key Numbers**: Before arriving, save all essential emergency contacts and download apps that may require internet access for initial setup.
2. **Carry a Backup Guide**: In case of technology failures, keep a printed map or guidebook from the Cruz Bay Visitor Center.
3. **Check Compatibility**: Ensure your mobile phone plan includes coverage in the U.S. Virgin Islands or use local SIM cards for affordable connectivity.

With these resources and tools, you'll be well-equipped to explore St. John confidently and safely, making the most of every moment on this idyllic island.